Bluegrass B
for the
Complete Ignoramus!

by
Wayne Erbsen

Order Number: NGB-104

ISBN 978-1-883206-44-4

Come visit us on the web at www.nativeground.com

IOU

Big thanks goes out to family, friends, students and fellow ignoramuses who have helped to shape this book: Barbara Swell, David Currier, Sally Wingate, Bob Buckingham, Jennifer Abbott, Mary Cowart, Corrine Glesne, Jerry Freeman, Barbara Osment, Elisa Litsky, and Bobby Anderson. Thanks to Doug Elliott for groundhog information, Wade Mainer, David Holt, Martin Liebschner and Paul Kuczko for generously loaning photographs and to the late Gus Meade for song research. Prolonged thanks for careful proofreading and valuable suggestions to Jon Singleton and Pete Vigour. Pete coined the term "drone string." Thanks guys!

Photo Credits: Steve Millard cover, p. 5; Everette Carpenter p. 1, 4; University of North Carolina at Chapel Hill p. 2, 26, 29, 39, 43, 56; Music Hall collection (Martin E. Liebschner Jr.) p. 5, 14, 20; French Kirkpatrick p. 6; Valentine Museum p. 8, 33; Jim Shumate p. 8; Paul Kuczko p. 10; photo by Jim Carr p. 16; Mars Hill College p. 16, 22; Bonnie & Rik Neustein p. 19; Warren Wilson College archive p. 35; Georgia Department of Archives & History p. 37; Berea College p. 38, 42; Wade Mainer & David Holt 41; Great Smoky National Park p. 47; photo by Wayne Erbsen p. 49; author's collection p. 17, 18, 44, 45, 51, 53, 54, 60; Ferrum College p. 63.

Dock Walsh

Instructional CD

To better help you learn the songs in this book, an instructional CD has been provided, which you'll find in a sleeve on the front inside cover. On the CD will be 99 cuts that correspond to the songs we'll be learning. For each song there will be three or four tracks to illustrate how to play the bare-bones melody using a variety of rolls, depending on your skill level. When you see the phonograph with the number inside, play that selection on your CD player so you can hear what we're talking about.

Contents

	Page Number	Track Number
Parts of a Banjo(ist)	4	
From One Ignoramus to Another	5	
How to Use this Book	6	
How to Buy a Banjo	7	
How to Hold Your Banjo	8	
Tuning for Ignoramuses	9	1
Fingering the Banjo	10	
How to Read Banjo Tablature	11	2
Playing Rolls	12	
Your First Roll, the Pinch	12	3
Melody Notes	13	
Drone Notes	13	
Yankee Doodle	13	4
Bile 'Em Cabbage Down	14	5, 6, 7, 8
Down the Road	16	9, 10, 11, 12
Groundhog	18	13, 14, 15, 16
Lynchburg Town	20	17, 18, 19
Poor Ellen Smith	22	20, 21, 22, 23
Palms of Victory	24	24, 25, 26, 27
Nine Pound Hammer	26	28, 29, 30
Columbus Stockade Blues	28	31, 32, 33
When I Lay My Burden Down	30	34, 35, 36, 37
Blue Ridge Mountain Blues	32	38, 39, 40, 41
Roll in My Sweet Baby's Arms	34	42, 43, 44
Wabash Cannonball	36	45, 46, 47
Red River Valley	38	48, 49, 50, 51
Little Maggie	40	52, 53, 54
Long Journey Home	42	55, 56, 57, 58
My Home's Across Blue Ridge Mtns	44	59, 60, 61, 62
Pass Me Not	46	63, 64, 65, 66
Pretty Polly	48	67, 68
Put My Little Shoes Away	50	69, 70, 71, 72
Shall We Gather at the River	52	73, 74, 75
When the Saints Go Marching In	54	76, 77, 78, 79
Man of Constant Sorrow	56	80, 81, 82, 83, 84
Beginning Rolls	58	85, 86, 87, 88
Forward Roll	59	89, 90
More Rolls	60	91, 92
Slides	61	93, 94, 95, 96, 97, 98, 99
Banjo Chords	62	
Native Ground Books & Music	64	

NOW AVAILABLE: **Companion to Bluegrass Banjo for the Complete Ignoramus!**
This hands-on Workbook will be the secret sauce for perking up your picking.

Parts of a Banjo(ist)

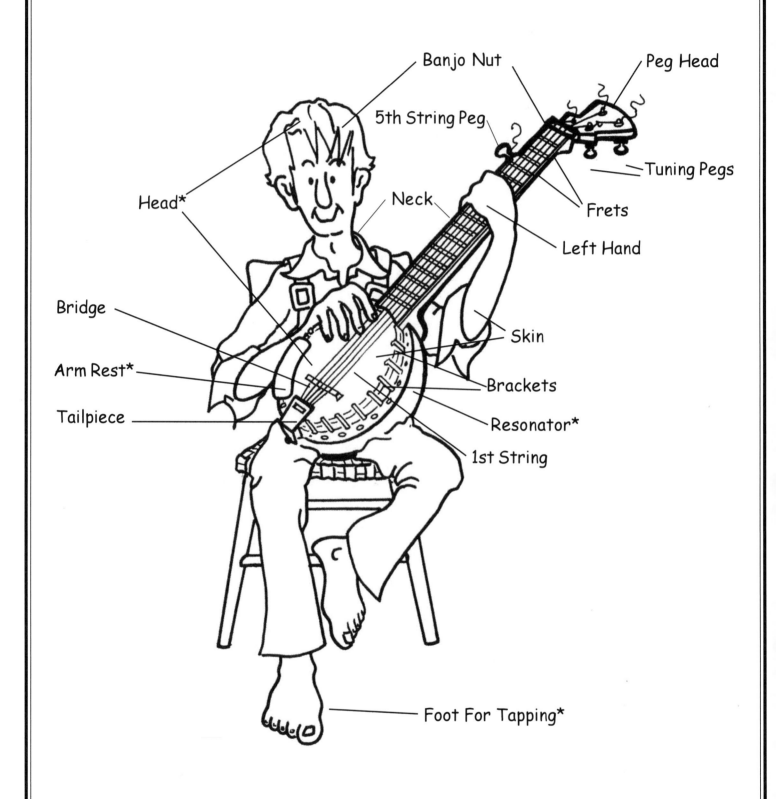

Banjo Nut

Peg Head

5th String Peg

Tuning Pegs

Head*

Neck

Frets

Left Hand

Bridge

Skin

Arm Rest*

Brackets

Tailpiece

Resonator*

1st String

Foot For Tapping*

Legend: * = optional

From One Ignoramus to Another

I didn't just ride into town in the back of a turnip truck, and neither did you. I've practically been at this banjo teaching business since dinosaurs roamed the earth. (Well, actually, it might have been 1963.) And my guess is that you've had the hankering to play the banjo since before dirt was invented. I'll even bet this is NOT the first banjo book you've picked up. With a little luck, a lot of gumption, and some stick-to-it-ivness on your part, it may be the last.

Nice to meet you.

Just so you'll feel you've bought the right book, I'll tell you that I've taught thousands and thousands of people to play the banjo. That's not even counting all the people who have learned from my five previous banjo books. My specialty is teaching TOTAL BEGINNERS. We're talking now about those who have never touched a banjo, about castoffs from other banjo teachers and people who all but quit believing in their dream of playing the banjo. To be blunt, we're talking about the flotsam and jetsam of the banjo world who have been washed ashore, limp with failure.

If you're one of those people who feels defeated by the banjo, you've come to the right place. If you've tried other books, teachers, workshops, and videos without luck, you have arrived at your destination. If banjo playing zigged when you zagged, you have entered the right door.

Take that chair right over there by the window.

In order to be successful with this book, you have to know exactly one thing: nuthin'! You don't even have to suspect anything. All you need is a banjo and the determination to learn how to pick it. I'll take care of the rest.

By now, you're probably wondering why am I so sure I can teach an ignoramus like you to play the banjo.

Because down deep, behind the fancy banjo, I'm an ignoramus too. It takes one to know one. It's as simple as that!

How to Use This Book

As you'll see when you thumb through this book, there's a certain amount of "fluffy" material at the beginning, such as how to pick out a banjo, what picks to use, how to hold the banjo, etc. Then the fluff stops and the guts take over. The real heart and soul of the book are the painfully simple tunes written out in banjo tablature. The tunes are laid bare and naked for you to look at and play. There's no fancy stuff cluttering up the basic starkness of the melodies.

That's the way it should be.

What I've given you are the essential melody notes to play the tune. Nothing more, nothing less. I call this the "skeleton" of the tune. No clothes, no nothin'. Then, in a separate closet, I give you simple rolls or clothes to "dress" the skeleton. (Heaven forbid you'd let a naked skeleton run around!)

The beauty of this method is that it's simple. It teaches you the basic melody for each song and then shows you how to add appropriate rolls to fill out the melody here and there. By approaching it in this way, you will quickly learn to improvise. You'll easily understand how to make up your own arrangements of the songs.

William Kirkpatrick, ca. 1920

Along with each song will be instructions for adding rolls to dress the melody. The easiest way to play it will be called "Ice Cold Licks." From there, things gradually progress in difficulty to "Cool Licks," "Warm Licks, " "Hot Licks," "Red Hot Licks," and even "White Hot Licks."

If you are a true ignoramus, I strongly advise you to go through the entire book just playing the ice cold and cool licks. When you can play all the songs with the simple rolls, then GRADUALLY turn up the heat. There's no use overwhelming yourself with the hot licks until you're ready for them. By and by, you'll really be cookin'!

How to Buy a Banjo

If you don't yet have a banjo, it might be a good idea to check with a local music store and see if they have rental banjos. If they rent banjos at a reasonable price, that might be a good way to "test the banjo waters." If you decide to take the big leap and buy one, here are some tips to help you. Keep in mind that it's usually easy to get back at least what you paid for a banjo, and in most cases, they're fairly easy to sell.

Strings. You are shopping for a 5-string banjo. 4-string banjos are used in Celtic or dixieland music and won't work for bluegrass or old-time music.

Resonator. You'll find that most banjos come equipped with a back or resonator. The resonator makes the banjo heavier, louder and often more flashy. As a beginner, you actually don't need a resonator, but most banjos will come with them anyway. If you find and fall in love with a great old banjo without a resonator, grab it. You can always get a second banjo with a resonator when you turn pro.

The Neck. It is critical that the banjo neck is straight, not warped or bowed. Hold the banjo up to your nose and sight down the neck along the fingerboard. Compare the straightness of the fingerboard with the strings that run parallel to it. If there is a dip or bow in the neck, either don't buy it or ask the salesman to see if it can be adjusted until it's straight.

Tuning Pegs. Most new banjos come with tuning pegs that are at least adequate, so don't be too concerned with this right now. The one weak point in many banjos is the 5th peg, which can be temperamental, at best. You can always add a new geared 5th string tuner at some later point if this one gets cantankerous. If the 5th string peg slips, try tightening the little screw on the end of the peg.

Action. "Action" is a two dollar word for the height of the strings. The higher the strings, the harder it is to play. However, if the strings are too low, they will rattle and buzz. The action is easy to adjust, so if you buy from a store, ask them to set the action at the right height before you walk out with it.

Tone. To me, all banjos sound great. After you get some experience, you'll develop your own ideas about what makes a good sounding banjo. In the meantime, I suggest you play as many banjos as you can get your hands on. You'll probably discover that the more expensive banjos tend to ring more, but, to me, even the lowliest banjo sounds just fine.

When you're shopping for a banjo, take a banjo pickin' friend with you and go to every music store in your area. Look at banjos in different price ranges, but remember that a relatively inexpensive banjo can be set up to play just as easily as a high dollar model. After you compare banjos from different stores you'll be in a better position to bargain for a better price. As you're comparing different banjos, think about them as you would a piece of furniture that you're buying for your house. Do you like the way it looks, hefts, smells, sounds? If you like antiques, hunt for a vintage banjo.

How to Hold Your Banjo

The banjo can be a slippery instrument, tricky to hold. A good way to hold it is to set it on your lap, between your legs with the neck pointing slightly upward. Push down on the armrest with your right forearm to help anchor the banjo in place. Your goal is for the banjo to stay put without having to hold it up with your left hand.

Many beginning banjo players soon find that their left arm gets tired while playing the banjo. A good set of barbells will strengthen your arm, but an easier solution is just to shift the banjo over to your right leg, as shown in this old photo taken in the late 19th century. This is how you want to look, ragged clothes, hat and all!

Earl Scruggs

It's not a bad idea to get a strap to help hold the banjo, although it's certainly not required. I recommend attaching the left end of the strap on the first bracket under the neck. You can attach the right end of the strap to one of the brackets near the tailpiece. Notice in this photo how a young Earl Scruggs rests his strap over his right shoulder. There's no telling how many thousands of banjo players have copied the way Earl held his banjo. If you try this, you'll soon find out it's rather awkward and uncomfortable to follow Earl's example. Why did he do it? It's actually hilarious to know that during a normal Flatt & Scruggs show, Earl would switch between the banjo and the guitar. The reason he put his strap over his right shoulder, instead of over his head, is that he didn't want to take off his hat! Unless you find yourself in the same pickle, I'd recommend putting the strap over your head so it rests on your left shoulder.

Tuning for Ignoramuses

Before we do anything else, let's get our banjos in tune. Tuning is a matter of patience and practice, so don't panic if you can't seem to get your darn banjo in tune at first. I can tell by looking at you that you don't have a tin ear, so let's learn to tune.

There are several methods of tuning your banjo. Keep in mind that the strings are numbered 1 - 5, with the 1st string being closest to the floor, and the 5th (or shorter) string being closest to your nose.

> ### Your Notes in G Tuning
> ## 1 = D, 2 = B, 3 = G, 4 = D, 5 = G

1. ELECTRONIC TUNER. If you're a true ignoramus who has never played a musical instrument before now, you just might want to invest in an electronic tuner. Simply tune to the notes in the box above.

2. PITCH PIPE. A less expensive alternative to an electronic tuner is a pitch pipe. Before you walk out of the music store with a pitch pipe, make sure it has the notes you'll need: D, B, and G.

3. PIANO. Not quite as portable as an electronic tuner or pitch pipe, a tuned piano is a dandy instrument to tune your banjo to. Again, tune your banjo to the notes in the box above.

4. GUITAR. The 2nd, 3rd, and 4th string of a guitar match those same strings of the banjo in G tuning. The 2nd string of the guitar fretted at the third fret will give you the pitch of your 1st or D string on the banjo. The 1st string of the guitar fretted at the third fret should sound like your 5th, or G string.

5. TUNING THE BANJO TO ITSELF. The most common (and best) method is to tune the banjo to itself. Pretend your 1st string is in tune (or tune it to a D from another tuned instrument or an electronic tuner). Then fret the 2nd string at the third fret and make the 2nd string sound like the 1st string played open, or unfretted. After you have matched the 2nd string to the 1st string, fret the 3rd string at the fourth fret and change the 3rd string until it matches the 2nd string played open. Then fret the 4th string at the fifth fret and adjust it until it sounds like the 3rd string played open. Finally, fret the 1st string at the fifth fret and tune your 5th string to it. That's it!

IMPORTANT TUNING TIP: Always sound the string as you are turning the peg. That way, you can tell how much the string is changing, and it's less likely to break!

Fingering the Banjo

YOUR RIGHT HAND: The fingers of your right hand have the simple but vital task of actually playing the notes. For your right hand, there's not much guesswork. For now, your thumb will hit the 2nd, 3rd, 4th, and 5th strings. It will never hit the 1st string. Your middle finger's sole responsibility will be to play the 1st string. We're not going to start out using the index finger but when we do, it will play the 2nd, 3rd, or, on rare occasions, the 4th string.

Be sure to rest at least your pinky down on the head or skin of the banjo to steady your right hand. Earl Scruggs, the master, recommends keeping both the ring finger and pinky down on the head, but that doesn't work for me. Whether you use one or two fingers, the point is that you need to anchor your hand by keeping a finger or two firmly planted on the head.

PICKS: Since you're still in the early stages of learning, I wouldn't bother with picks at this point. Picks help you play louder and faster, neither of which is a bonus right now! When you're ready to try picks, I'd recommend heavy gauge Dunlop fingerpicks and a plastic thumb pick. The fingerpicks are used on your index and middle fingers and are turned so they cover the end of your finger opposite your fingernail.

YOUR LEFT HAND: The fingers of your left hand are going to have to learn to think for themselves. (Eeeeks.) They will constantly have to choose amongst themselves which one's going to go where.

Just as you probably wouldn't type with one finger (as I'm doing), you also wouldn't want to fret all the strings with just one finger. The basic rule is to use a different finger when you play a different fret. If you skip a fret, skip a finger. In this book the most common type of song uses frets one, two, three and occasionally four. In this case, use your index finger for the first fret, your middle finger for the second fret, and your ring finger for the third fret. If you need to play the fourth fret, either use your ring finger, or better yet, reach up there with your pinky. The pinky is definitely the runt of the litter and the weakest of the bunch, too. Using it will make it tough, like the big boys.

How to Read Banjo Tablature

Instead of standard musical notation, banjo players use a system called "tablature" to write out the music. It's how they communicate with their own kind. Trust me, it's really quite easy to read.

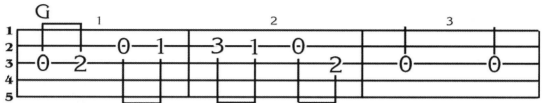

In the example above, you'll see five horizontal lines. These are your five strings of the banjo, which are numbered on the left side. The numbers on the lines or strings represent the frets that you play on that string. For example, an "O" on the middle line would mean you play the 3rd string "open" or unfretted. A "2" on the middle line would mean you press down or "fret" the 3rd string at the second fret. This activity is called "fretting." Remember to use the tips of fingers and to play about half-way between the medal frets. Above each measure is a tiny number. These numbers just identify the measure, so you and I will know what measure we're referring to as we talk amongst ourselves as we wander through the book. The number in the phonograph tells you what track of the CD to listen to.

If you play the notes in the example above, you discover you're playing part of a G scale that goes up and back down again. To get the timing right, you can use your foot as a metronome. Where the notes are tied together, like the "O" and the "2" at the very beginning of the line, your foot would go "down up," as in the following illustration. As your foot hits the floor, you would play the 3rd string open or unfretted. When your foot comes up, you would play the 3rd string at the second fret.

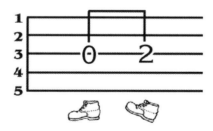

On the notes that are all by themselves with a single stem, as in the following example, each of those notes would get a "down up" with your foot.

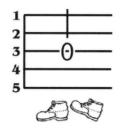

Playing Rolls

The thing that sets bluegrass banjo playing apart from any other type of music is the way that the banjo uses rolls to play the melody. A roll is nothing more than a series or pattern of notes. The rolls become your tools, like a hammer or a saw. In this book we're going to learn to play the melody using a toolbox full of seven basic rolls: the pinch, the two-finger roll, the pegleg sailor roll, the alternating thumb roll, the forward roll, the reverse roll and the "Foggy Mountain Breakdown" roll.

What's unique about this book is that I'm not going to present the tunes with the rolls already incorporated into the song. Instead, you'll get just the bare-bones skeleton of the tune. With my help, you'll learn how to dress the skeleton with this roll or that one. The beauty of this method is that you can dress the skeleton whichever way YOU want to. It means YOU DON'T HAVE TO PLAY IT THE SAME WAY TWICE. Excuse me for yelling, but this is important, and I was afraid you might not hear it. Once you get into the swing of the book, you'll start to realize how much sense this method makes. If you don't, send it back, and I'll return your money.

Your First Roll: the Pinch

I call this first roll "the pinch." It will soon become your best friend because 1) it's easy, 2) it's versatile, and 3) you can plug it in just about anywhere.

The pinch is nothing more than plucking the 1st and 5th strings together at the same time. Use your middle finger on the 1st string and your thumb on the 5th string. Here's the way it works: you'll play a melody note on the 2nd, 3rd, or 4th string with your thumb and then the pinch. Let's try it. Play the 2nd string followed by the pinch, then the 3rd followed by a pinch, and finally the 4th string followed by the pinch. In tablature, it looks like this:

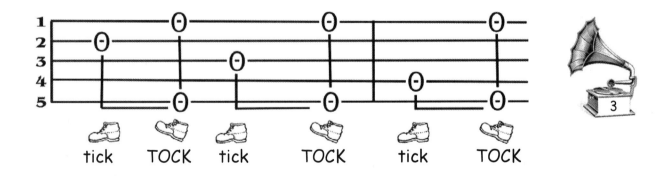

In this example, the melody is represented by a "tick" on the 2nd, 3rd and 4th strings. Each melody note gets a DOWN with your foot and each pinch gets an UP with your foot. Practice hitting the 2nd, 3rd and 4th strings in any order with your thumb while you quickly follow each note with a pinch. The rhythm should sound like one TWO, one TWO or tick TOCK, tick TOCK.

Melody Notes

In the tablature in this book there are only two kinds of melody notes: single melody notes and two melody notes tied together. Examples of the single notes can be found on the following page on the song "Bile 'Em Cabbage Down." Two notes tied together is illustrated below on the song "Yankee Doodle."

SINGLE MELODY NOTES: After each of the single melody notes of "Bile 'Em Cabbage Down" you'll need to play a roll of your choice. Keep in mind that for each measure, up to eight notes can be played. Some of the rolls you'll be learning have the equivalent of four notes: these include the pinch, two-finger picking, the pegleg sailor roll and the alternating thumb roll. More advanced rolls will have as many as eight notes. These rolls would include the forward roll, reverse and the "Foggy Mountain Breakdown" roll. Each of these rolls is explained near the back of the book on pages 58-60.

Drone Notes

Alongside the rolls is another tool that will form the basis of bluegrass banjo playing: drone notes. Drone notes are quick little notes that are always played on the 1st string and are used to fill in around the melody notes that are tied together. Below is a fragment of the well-known tune "Yankee Doodle." Try picking out the tune with your right thumb.

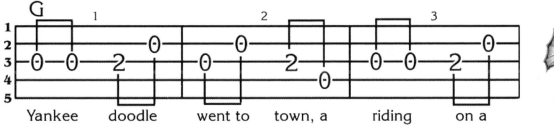 

This time play "Yankee Doodle" with a drone note (1st string played open with your right middle finger) AFTER each melody note. Keep in mind that the drone notes are optional. You can play them when you want. It's often a good idea to leave off the last drone note in a measure to give you breathing space before launching into a new measure. Leaving off the last drone note also gives a blessed moment of silence before a new melody note is played. The silence will help "frame" the next melody note, making it stand out more.

Here is the first measure of "Yankee Doodle," with each of the drone notes shown. Note that there are now a full eight notes per measure, the MOST that can be played in this book.

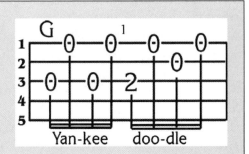

Bile 'Em Cabbage Down

"Bile 'Em Cabbage Down" is a minstrel tune from the 1850s that is a great tune to start with. For those of you who don't speak "Southern," the word "bile" in the title means "boil." The verses float from song to song and can be found in such songs as "Shady Grove," "Whoa Mule," and "Lynchburg Town," among others. The "hoe cakes" mentioned in the song were a favorite in the antebellum South. Slaves often cooked corn meal hoe cakes on their hoes over an open fire. Confederate soldiers reportedly roasted them on bayonets.

You'll notice chords above each of the lines of the tablature. When you're first starting off, you can ignore those chords. After you get to where you can play the tune using the warm licks, you can add the chords (see page 62).

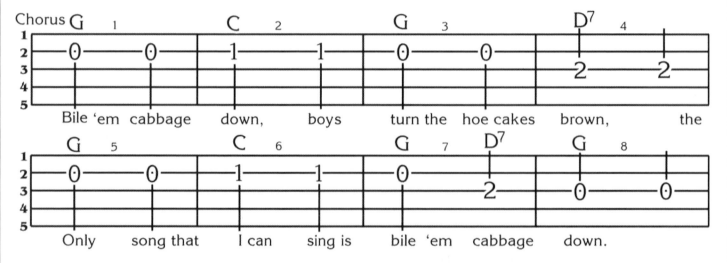

Went up on the mountain,
Give my horn a blow.
Thought I heard my true love say,
Yonder stands my beau. (Chorus)

Went to see my gal last night,
I done it kind a-sneakin'.
Kissed her mouth and hit her nose,
And the doggone thing was leakin'. (Chorus)

Jaybird died with the whooping cough,
Sparrow died with the colic.
Along come the frog with a fiddle on his back,
Inquirin' his way to the frolic. (Chorus)

Took my gal to the blacksmith shop,
To have her mouth made small.
She turned around a time or two,
And swallowed the shop and all. (Chorus)

The bare-bones skeleton of "Bile 'Em Cabbage Down" on page 14 is as simple as bluegrass banjo gets! With practice and time, you'll gain experience and confidence and will gradually be able to play the same melody with a variety of rolls. In effect, you'll be dressing the skeleton with clothes of your choosing. What follows are some of the clothes you can use to dress your melody. As you go down the page, the rolls will get progressively harder. Don't be in a big hurry to play it as fancy as you can. LESS IS MORE. Be sure you can play the cold licks before progressing to the warm and hot licks. In fact, if you're a true ignoramus, it would be wise to play all or most of the songs in the book using the cold licks. Then go through the book playing the warm licks, and finally, the hot licks. But since this is your workbook and nobody's looking over your shoulder (yet!), you can progress at your own speed.

ICE COLD LICKS: First, play just the chorus melody of "Bile 'Em Cabbage Down" with your right thumb. Notice that all the melody notes are either on the 2nd or the 3rd strings. Make sure to use the index finger of your left hand to play the first fret notes, and your middle finger to play the second fret notes. For now, ignore the chords.

COOL LICKS: When you can play the melody of "Bile 'Em Cabbage Down" blindfolded, standing on one leg, while chewing gum and reciting the Pledge of Allegiance, you're ready to add the pinch. After each of the melody notes simply play the 1st and 5th strings together with your middle finger and thumb.

WARM LICKS: Add the C chord where indicated. (See page 62.)

EVEN WARMER LICKS: Instead of playing the pinch, play the two-finger roll. (2 1 5 1 or 3 1 5 1. See page 58.) With your thumb playing the melody, try alternating the pinch with the two-finger roll. For variety, play the pegleg sailor roll instead of the two-finger roll (page 58).

HOT LICKS: After you've mastered this tune with all the above rolls, you may be ready to try using the forward roll (page 59). Start off each forward roll with your index finger. Notice that on measure four the melody moves to the 3rd string, so your roll would be 3 1 5 3 1 5 3 1. Remember, the last note is optional. Line two starts off like line one until measure seven, where we have something new. The melody moves from the 2nd string to the 3rd string. When using the forward roll in a situation like this, you'll of course start out with your index finger playing the 2nd string. You'll play 2 1 5. Now, since the melody moves to the 3rd string, you'll fret the 3rd string at the second fret and play 3 1 5 3 1. So the entire roll would be 2 1 5 3 1 5 3 1. Measure eight is a good place to use pinches after each of the melody notes.

After you're comfortable playing this tune using your index finger to lead off the forward roll, you can try it using your thumb. Remember, you'll use the thumb only on the first of the eight note roll. On the fourth note, you'll continue to use your index finger.

Down the Road

I always look forward to teaching "Down the Road" because it's one of those songs that sounds great, and is also relatively easy to play. The first recording of "Down the Road" that caught my attention was the hot version by Flatt & Scruggs. Lester Flatt did a great job on the singing, but he didn't sing a chorus. The Greenbriar Boys came along in the early 1960s and recorded it with a chorus that we're going to play on the banjo.

It was many years after I first learned "Down the Road" that I realized the song was much older than the Flatt & Scruggs version. Uncle Dave Macon recorded a rousing rendition on July 25, 1928 that he called "Over the Road I'm Bound to Go." The melody is basically the same as the tune "Ida Red," which was first recorded by Fiddlin' Powers & Family on August 19, 1924.

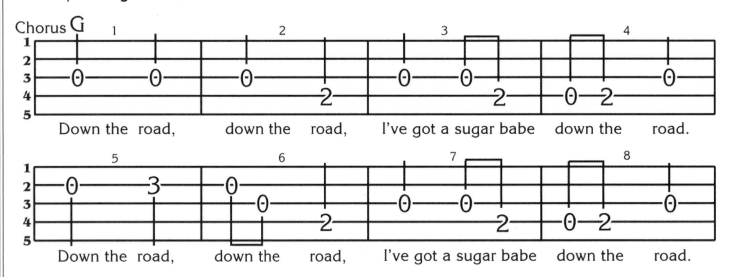

Down the road, down the road, I've got a sugar babe down the road.

Down the road, down the road, I've got a sugar babe down the road.

Down the road about a mile or two
Lives a little girl named Pearly Blue.
About so high and her hair is brown,
Prettiest girl, boys, in this town. (Chorus)

Anytime you want to know
Where I'm going down the road.
Get my girl on the line,
You can find me there most anytime. (Chorus)

Every day and Sunday too
I go see my Pearly Blue.
Soon as you hear the rooster crow,
You can see me heading down the road. (Chorus)

Every time I get the blues
I walk the sole right off my shoes.
Don't know why I love her so,
That girl of mine lives down the road. (Chorus)

Snuffy Jenkins

16

Ice Cold - Red Hot Licks

ICE COLD LICKS: Go through the tune and play the melody of "Down the Road" with your thumb. Make sure to use your middle finger of your left hand to play the notes on the second fret, and your ring finger to play the notes on the third fret.

COOL LICKS: When you can play the melody without looking at the book, add drone notes (see page 13) in measures three, four, six, seven and eight. After each lone melody note, play the pinch. (See page 58) .

WARM LICKS: Instead of playing the pinch, play the two-finger roll. (2 1 5 1, 3 1 5 1 or 4 1 5 1. See page 58.)

With your thumb playing the melody, try alternating the pinch with the two-finger roll.

For variety, play the pegleg sailor roll (2 _ 5 1 or 3 _ 5 1 or 4 _ 5 1. See page 58) instead of the two-finger roll. Alternate it with the pinch.

HOT LICKS: This is a good tune to try out the alternating thumb roll that is explained on page 58. Every time there is a note by itself on the 3rd or 4th strings (like the first four notes in measures one and two), play the alternating thumb roll. So, for the first note of this song (the 3rd string played open) you'll play 3 2 5 1 using your thumb on the 3, your index finger on the 2, your thumb on the 5, and your middle finger on the 1. Remember that when the melody goes up to the 2nd string (as in measure five) use either your pinch or two-finger roll. .

RED HOT LICKS: Just for kicks, you can add a slide at the beginning of the tune. (See page 61). To do this, you'll have to modify your alternating thumb roll so instead of playing 3 2 5 1, you're now playing 4 3 5 1. Use the same fingers you used before, which is thumb, index finger, thumb, middle finger. Instead of playing the 3rd string open at the beginning of the song, now you can hit the 4th string, but you'll do a slide from the 4th string at the second fret to the 4th string at the fifth fret. Right after you do the slide, you'll play 3 5 1.

As you go through the song, occasionally substitute the pinch for the alternating thumb roll on the notes that are by themselves.

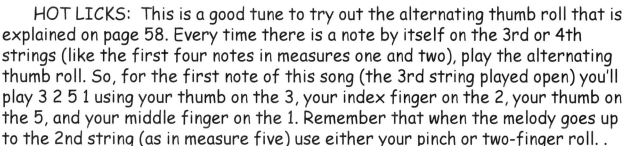

Groundhog

Y ou'll find "Groundhog" a great tune which is commonly played both in old-time and in bluegrass music. It's written in kind of a minor key, which produces a spooky or haunting sound.

When I perform the song "Groundhog," I like to explain to the audience that early old-time mountain banjos often used a groundhog skin for the head of the banjo. Of course, that was after the groundhog was the invited guest for supper! For mountain people, groundhogs provided more than meat on the table and skins for their banjos. Groundhog grease was a common remedy for croup and was applied to the skin as a liniment for arthritis. Groundhogs are often called whistlepigs because of their high-pitched whistle. In the north, groundhogs are known as woodchucks. Out west, they're related to the marmot or rockchuck.

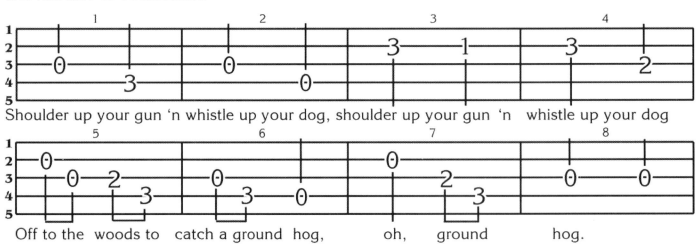

Shoulder up your gun 'n whistle up your dog, shoulder up your gun 'n whistle up your dog

Off to the woods to catch a ground hog, oh, ground hog.

Here comes Sal with a great long pole,
Here comes Sal with a great long pole,
Twist that whistlepig outta his hole,
Oh, groundhog.

Here comes Sal with a snigger and a grin,
Here comes Sal with a snigger and a grin,
Ground hog grease all over her chin,
Oh, groundhog.

Here comes grannie hopping on a cane,
Here comes grannie hopping on a cane,
Said, "I'm gonna eat that groundhog's brain,"
Oh, groundhog.

Groundhog stewed and ground hog fried,
Groundhog stewed and ground hog fried,
It's the best old groundhog ever I tried,
Oh, groundhog.

We'll catch a groundhog and save his hide,
We'll catch a groundhog and save his hide,
It'll make the best shoestrings you ever tied,
Oh, groundhog.

Take this song and put it on the shelf
Take this song and put it on the shelf,
If you want any more you can sing it yourself,
Oh, groundhog.

Ice Cold - Red Hot Licks

ICE COLD LICKS: The first thing to do is to play through the bare-bones melody of "Groundhog" using just your right thumb. When fretting the notes with your left hand, I suggest using your ring finger to play the third fret notes, your index finger to play the first fret notes, and your middle finger to play the second fret notes. After you've gone through "Groundhog" several times playing the naked melody, add drone notes after the notes that are tied together.

COOL LICKS: Once you can play the basic melody of "Groundhog" without looking at the tablature, you're ready to add the pinch after each lone melody note. (See page 58 on the pinch).

Before turning up the temperature by advancing on to the warmer licks, make sure you can play "Groundhog" using the pinch and the drone notes. This song shouldn't be played too fast. Your goal should be to play it at a nice even tempo so you don't pause or slow down over any difficult spots and speed up over the easy parts.

WARM LICKS: In place of the pinch you can try the two-finger roll (2 1 5 1, 3 1 5 1 or 4 1 5 1. See page 58). When you've got that, alternate the two-finger roll with the pinch. For spice you can occasionally throw in the pegleg sailor roll (page 58).

HOT LICKS: Measures one and two are a good place to use your alternating thumb roll (page 58). On measure one you'd play 3 2 5 1 followed by 4 2 5 1. Of course, you'd fret the 4th string at the third fret. On measure three the melody moves up to the 2nd string, so there you would play the pinch or two-finger roll. At the end of measure four you can play the second fret note with the pinch or the two-finger roll. If you want to play the second fret note with the alternating thumb roll, you'll need to make a D7 chord. (See page 62).

WHITE HOT LICKS: The first two measures of "Groundhog" are a dandy places to try using a slide with your alternating thumb roll (See page 61). Instead of playing the 3rd string open at the beginning of measure one, fret the 4th string at the third fret and slide up to the fifth fret. Then quickly play the rest of the alternating thumb roll. The entire roll would be 4 3 5 1. Instead of playing the open 3rd string at the beginning of measure two, you can slide from the third fret in measure one, going up to the fifth fret using your alternating thumb roll.

Lynchburg Town

I first learned "Lynchburg Town" back in the early 1960s from a group called the Louisiana Honeydrippers. Although the tune is hard to trace, I suspect it goes back to before the Civil War. It was first recorded by Gid Tanner and Riley Puckett on September 11, 1924 under the title of "Going Along Down Town." Two years later the Blue Ridge Highballers recorded it as "Going Down to Lynchburg Town." Other interesting names for the tune are "Monkey Show," "The Old Hat," and "Going Down to Corbin Town."

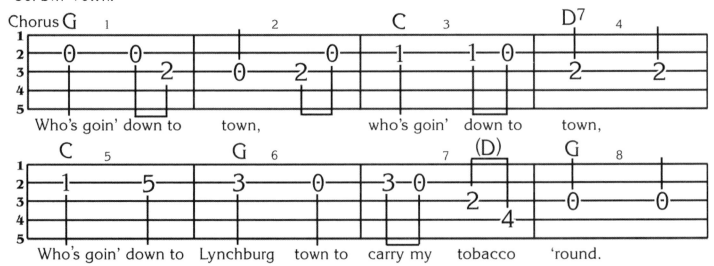

Who's goin' down to town, who's goin' down to town,
Who's goin' down to Lynchburg town to carry my tobacco 'round.

Once I had an old big dog
I wished they'd bring him back
Run them big hogs over the fence
And the little ones through the cracks. (Chorus)

Well, I married a little gal
And I brought her from the South
She balled her hair so doggone tight
She couldn't shut her mouth. (Chorus)

Possum up a 'simmon tree
Raccoon on the ground
Raccoon said, you son of a gun,
Throw them 'simmons down. (Chorus)

Possom shake the tree
'Simmons start to fall
Raccoon said, "you doggone fool,
I didn't want 'em all!" (Chorus)

Johnson had an old grey horse
His name was Martin Brown
Every foot old Martin had
Would cover an acre of ground. (Chorus)

Note: In measure 7 the D is in parentheses because you only need to finger two notes of the D chord: the 3rd string at the second fret and the 4th string at the fourth fret.

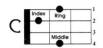 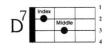

ICE COLD LICKS: Play through "Lynchburg Town" just playing the melody with your thumb. In measures one and two be sure to use your middle finger of your left hand to play the 3rd string at the second fret. Of course, on measure three you would use your index finger to play the first fret notes. On measure five you need to fret the 2nd string at the first fret with your index finger and then your ring finger to play on the fifth fret. Then use your middle finger play the 2nd string at the third fret at the beginning of measure six. Measure seven is the only hard part of the song. You would play the third fret note with your middle finger, the second fret note with your index finger, and use your ring finger or pinky to play the fourth fret note.

COOL LICKS: Drone notes can be played after one or both of the notes that are tied together.

Now you can add the pinch (page 58) after any note that's standing by itself.

CHORDS: The chords on "Lynchburg Town" are more or less optional, but it wouldn't hurt to learn to play them. (See page 62). On measure three you'll need to go to a C. Measure four tells you to play a D7. If you're going to use a roll on measure four that includes the 2nd string, you'll need to play a complete D7 chord. Otherwise, you can just play a partial D7 by just playing the 3rd string at the second fret. On measure five you'll start out playing a C chord, but when the melody goes up to the fifth fret, you don't need to worry about the C. Trust me, it will sound fine.

WARM LICKS: Use the alternating thumb roll (3 2 5 1) on any measure where the note by itself is on the 3rd string. You'll find those at the beginning of measure two, both notes in measure four, and both notes in measure eight.

HOT LICKS: "Lynchburg Town" is a good tune to play the forward roll in several places (see page 59). On measure one you would start the forward roll on the 2nd string with your index finger, playing 2 1 5 2 1 5. Then, you would fret the 3rd string at the second fret and play the rest of the forward roll, which would be 3 1. In this case, the entire forward roll would be 2 1 5 2 1 5 3 1. Here it is written out for you. The letters at the bottom tell you the fingers of your right hand to use. "I" is the index finger, "M" is middle finger, and "T" is your thumb.

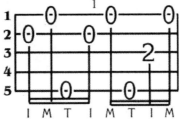

Measure three is another place you can use the forward roll. Here you would go to a C chord and simply play 215 215 21. On the last 2 you will have to take your left index finger off of the 2nd string at the first fret so you'll be playing that melody note open or unfretted.

Poor Ellen Smith

It's always fun when the tune you're playing has a story behind it, and this one has doozie. The lyrics were apparently written by Peter de Graff while awaiting execution by electric chair in 1893 for the murder of Ellen Smith. The melody was purloined from the hymn "How Firm a Foundation." The kicker is that it became a crime to sing the song in Forsyth County, North Carolina because tempers were running so hot after the trial that it always fomented a riot. No telling what they'd do to you if they caught you playing it on the banjo!

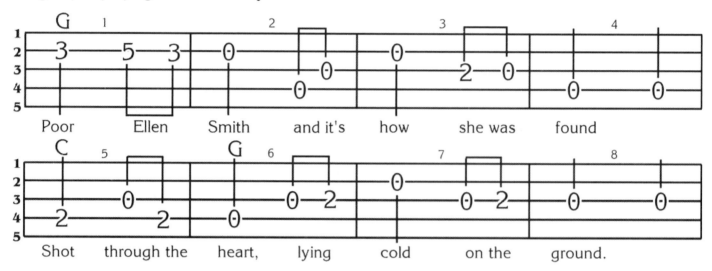

Her clothes were all scattered and thrown on the ground,
The blood marks the spot where poor Ellen was found.

They picked up their rifles and hunted me down,
They found me a-loafing all around the town.

They picked up her body and carried it away,
And now she is sleeping in some lonesome old grave.

I got a letter yesterday, I read it today,
The flowers on her grave have all faded away.

Someday I'll go home and say when I go,
On poor Ellen's grave pretty flowers I'll sow.

I've been in this prison for twenty long years,
Each night I see Ellen through my bitter tears.

The warden just told me that soon I'll be free,
To go to her grave 'neath that old willow tree.

My days in this prison are ending at last,
I'll never be free from the sins of my past.

Poor Ellen Smith how was she found,
Shot through the heart lying cold on the ground.

Samantha Bumgarner

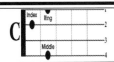

Ice Cold - Red Hot Licks

ICE COLD LICKS: Play just the melody of "Poor Ellen Smith." At the beginning of measure one I recommend using your left index finger to fret the third fret note. Leave your index finger there and play the fifth fret note with your ring finger or pinky. Now you'll play the third fret note again, but since you left your index finger there, it will be easy to play.

COOL LICKS: Play the drone notes after the notes that are tied together. Then try "Poor Ellen Smith" with the pinch. You can also play it with the two-finger roll (2 1 5 1, 3 1 5 1 or 4 1 5 1).

WARM LICKS: Anytime a single melody note is on the 3rd or 4th string, try your alternating thumb roll (3 2 5 1 or 4 2 5 1).

HOT LICKS: The first measure is a likely candidate (or victim!) for a forward roll. While fretting the 2nd string at the third, fifth and third frets, you'll play 2 1 5 2 1 5 2 1. Written out, it would look like this:

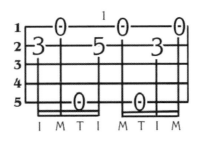

RED HOT LICKS: When you got "Poor Ellen Smith" nailed using your pinch, two-finger roll, alternating thumb roll and forward roll, you're ready to unleash the reverse roll (page 60). Since the reverse roll is limited to places where the melody is on the 3rd and 4th strings, the only place you can use it on "Poor Ellen Smith" is on measures four and eight.

Palms of Victory

Also known as "Deliverance Will Come," this old hymn was claimed by several composers but I'll put my money on the late Gus Meade's research that shows the true composer to be John B. Mathis, who wrote the words and music in 1836. Uncle Dave Macon was the first to record it, on September 8, 1926.

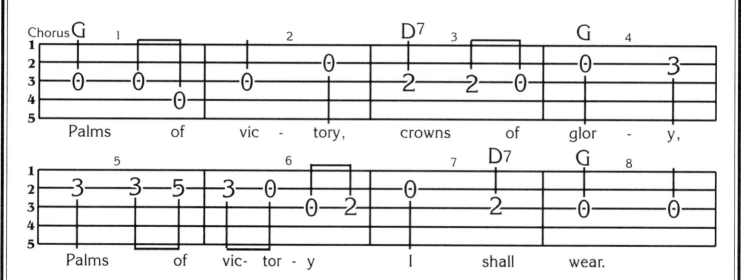

I saw a wayward traveler in tattered garments clad,
And struggling up the mountain, it seemed that he was sad.
His back was laden heavy, his strength was almost gone,
Yet he shouted as he journeyed, "Deliverance will come!" (Chorus)

The summer sun was shining, the sweat was on his brow,
His garments worn and dusty, his step seemed very slow.
But he kept pressing onward, for he was wending home,
Still shouting as he journeyed, "Deliverance will come!" (Chorus)

The songsters in the arbor, that stood beside the way,
Attracted his attention, inviting his delay.
His watchword being "Onward!" he stopped his ears and ran,
Still shouting as he journeyed, "Deliverance will come!" (Chorus)

I saw him in the evening, the sun was bending low,
He'd overtopped the mountain, and reached the vale below.
He saw the golden city, his everlasting home,
And shouted loud "Hosanna, Deliverance will come!" (Chorus)

While gazing on that city, just o'er that narrow flood,
A band of holy angels came from the throne of God.
They bore him on their pinions, safe o'er the dashing foam,
And joined him in his triumph, "Deliverance will come!" (Chorus)

I heard the song of triumph, they sang upon the shore,
Saying "Jesus has redeemed us, to suffer nevermore."
Then casting his eyes backward, on the race which he had run,
He shouted loud "Hosanna, Deliverance will come!" (Chorus)

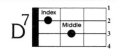

Ice Cold - Red Hot Licks

ICE COLD LICKS: When you play the melody of "Palms of Victory" be sure to use your index finger on the third fret notes at the beginning of line two and your ring finger or pinky on the fifth fret notes.

COOL LICKS: Now you can try playing "Palms of Victory" adding your drone notes and either a pinch or the two-finger roll (2 1 5 1 or 3 1 5 1) after each melody single melody note.

WARM LICKS: On any of the single melody notes on the 3rd string, you can play the alternating thumb roll (3 2 5 1). Mix it up with your pinches.

HOT LICKS: The first measure of "Palms of Victory" is a dandy place to play the forward roll. On the last part of the roll your index finger would drop down to the 4th string. The entire forward roll would then be 3 1 5 3 1 5 4 1.

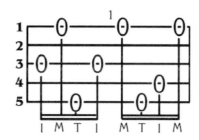

If you use the forward roll on measure one, as a contrast I'd use the pinch on measure two. On measure three, you can go back and use the forward roll: 3 1 5 3 1 5 3 1. Of course, the first two times you play the 3rd string you'll be fretting it at the second fret and the last time you'll play it open or unfretted. For contrast, on measure four you can use a pinch after each melody note.

RED HOT LICKS: Instead of using the forward roll on measure one and three, you might want to try what I call the "Foggy Mountain Breakdown" roll (see page 60). In this case, measure one would be 3 1 3 1 5 4 1 5.

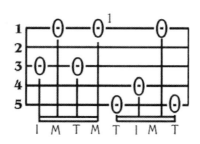

Nine Pound Hammer

Although they were not the first to record "Nine Pound Hammer," it was certainly the February 17, 1936 recording by Bill and Charlie Monroe who really put this song on the map. The song itself was not written from beginning to end by anyone we can point a finger to. Instead, it was pieced together out of a patchwork of fragments from both black and white sources.

The song we now call "Nine Pound Hammer" came to life with the May 13, 1927 recording in New York by Al Hopkins & His Buckle Busters. Years later, Hopkins admitted to folklorists Archie Green and Ed Kahn that the band pieced the song together in the New York studio of Brunswick records. Each member of the band added what random verses he could remember until the song was "recomposed" right before they recorded it. The recording in effect "froze" their collection of verses into the song we now know as "Nine Pound Hammer." Good work, boys!

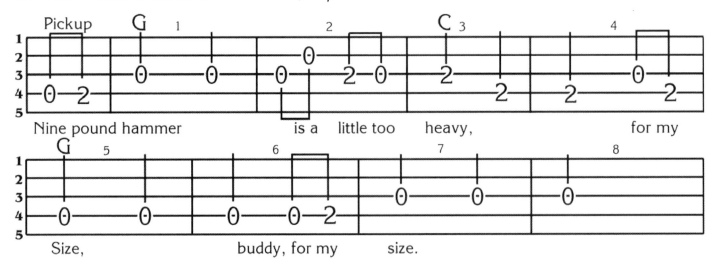

Chorus:
    Roll on buddy,
    Don't you roll so slow,
    Baby, how can I roll,
    When my wheel won't go?

Somebody stole
My nine pound hammer,
Baby, took it and gone,
Baby, took it and gone.

Nine pound hammer,
Killed John Henry,
Ain't a-gonna kill me,
Ain't a-gonna kill me.

Goin' on the mountain,
For to see my darlin'
And I ain't comin' back,
And I ain't coming' back.

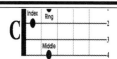

Ice Cold - Red Hot Licks

PICKUP NOTES: "Nine Pound Hammer is the first song we've had using what we call "pickup notes." These are notes that lead you into the first measure of the song, which is numbered with a "1."

ICE COLD LICKS: With all the melody notes of "Nine Pound Hammer" being either open strings or at the second fret, you'll find this tune very easy to play.

28

COOL LICKS: Play "Nine Pound Hammer" with the drone notes and the pinch.

29

WARM LICKS: Now use your alternating thumb roll on any single note that's on the 3rd or 4th strings (3 2 5 1 or 4 2 5 1). Mix in a pinch now and then. On measure three you'll need to hold down a C chord while you play the melody.

30

HOT LICKS: Measure one would be a good spot to use the reverse roll: 3 2 1 5 1 2 3 1.

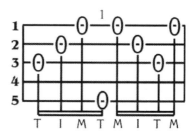

If you like, you can also use the reverse roll on measures three, five and seven.

91

Note: In measure three the melody is played on the 3rd string at the second fret. At the same time you play this melody note, you can also play a C chord (see page 62). To do this, you would make a C chord with your index and ring fingers and add your middle finger to the 3rd string at the second fret. To play the next melody note in measure three, keep your two-finger C chord and simply move your middle finger from the 3rd string at the second fret to the 4th string at the second fret. If you are an ignoramus on the banjo, ignore the C chord completely and just play the melody notes.

Columbus Stockade Blues

Tom Darby and Jimmy Tarlton had the first recording of "Columbus Stockade Blues" on November 10, 1927. It shares some of the lines of the folksong "Don't This Road Look Rough and Rocky," and the Carter Family song "Little Darling, Pal of Mine." The long list of people who have recorded it includes Carson Robison, Cliff Carlisle, Jimmie Davis and Bill Monroe.

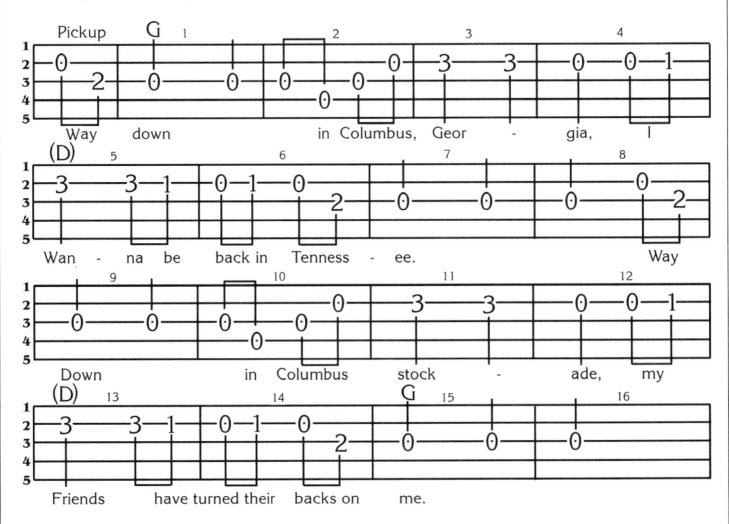

Chorus:

C
Go and leave me if you wish to,

G
Never let it cross your mind.

If in your heart you love another,

D7   G
Leave me little darlin', I don't mind.

Many a night with you I've rambled
Many an hour I've spent with you.
Thought I'd gained your heart forever
Though you have proved false to me. (Chorus)

Last night while I lay sleeping
I dreamed that I was in your arms.
When I awoke I was mistaken
I was peeping through the bars. (Chorus)

Note: Measures 5 and 13 show a D in parentheses. You can ignore the D and just play the melody. The Ds are there to show your back-up band the chords.

ICE COLD LICKS: Playing through the melody of "Columbus Stockade Blues" will be a snap and you'll barely have to move your left hand to reach all the notes. On measures five and six be sure to use your index finger to play the 2nd string at the first fret and your ring finger to play the 2nd string at the third fret. Memorizing "Columbus Stockade Blues" will be easy because lines three and four are the same as lines one and two.

COOL LICKS: Play a pinch on the single melody notes along with the drone notes where two notes are grouped together. Alternate the pinch with the two-finger roll on the single melody notes (2 1 5 1 or 3 1 5 1).

WARM LICKS: Use your alternating thumb roll on the single melody notes where the single melody notes are on the 3rd string (3 2 5 1). Mix it in with the pinch.

HOT LICKS: On measures one, seven, nine and fifteen, you can use either the reverse roll (3 2 1 5 1 2 3) or the "Foggy Mountain Breakdown" roll (3 1 3 1 5 3 1 5). Refer to page 60 for details on these rolls.

RED HOT LICKS: You'll find that measure three is a good place to play a forward roll (2 1 5 2 1 5 2 1). If you like, you can slide into the three at the beginning of the measure from the second fret.

Note: The D7 chord in parentheses is optional, so you can ignore it while playing the tune. When you're playing chords for backup, you can put it in.

Another Note: The chorus has a different melody and set of chords than the verses. If you can find someone to sing the chorus, merely play a simple roll (like the pinch) as you change chords. Eventually, you can substitute other rolls for the pinch. Your object is to keep the beat with your rolls while you change chords at the right place. Good luck!

When I Lay My Burden Down

Don't be fooled by the title, "When I Lay My Burden Down." The melody of this song is exactly the same as "Will The Circle Be Unbroken." That's the song I really wanted to teach you, but if I printed the lyrics to the commonly sung Carter Family version of "Will The Circle Be Unbroken," I'd have twenty-seven money-hungry attorneys banging at my door faster than I could spit and holler "Howdy." This is all because of Ralph Peer, who placed an ironclad copyright on every note the Carter Family sang. Pardon me if I sound a little bit testy over this issue. I am grateful to the Carter Family for gathering such great songs together to record. I only wish the law would allow me to teach them to willing students.

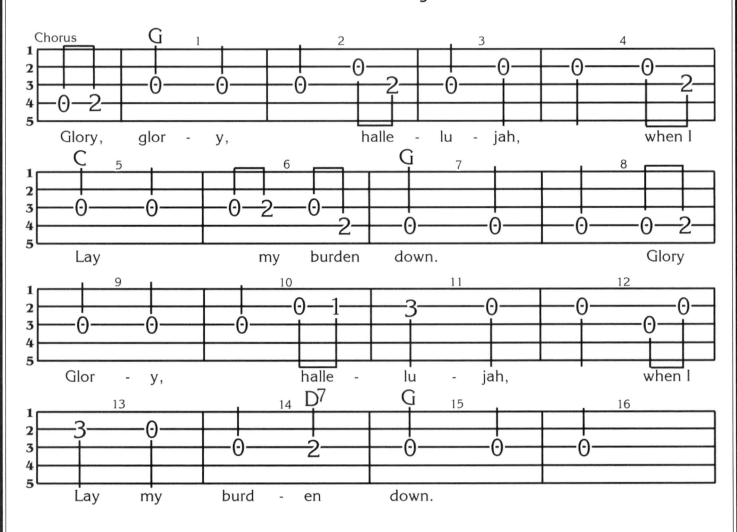

Oh I want to see my father,
When I lay my burden down.
Oh I want to see my father,
When I lay my burden down. (Chorus)

Oh I want to see my mother,
When I lay my burden down.
Oh I want to see my mother,
When I lay my burden down. (Chorus)

Oh I want to see my Jesus,
When I lay my burden down.
Oh I want to see my Jesus,
When I lay my burden down. (Chorus)

I am on my way to heaven.
When I lay my burden down.
I am on my way to heaven.
When I lay my burden down. (Chorus)

 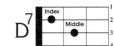

34

ICE COLD LICKS: Picking out the melody of "When I Lay My Burden Down" should be a piece of cake because all the notes are easy to get to. On measures eleven and thirteen be sure to use your ring finger to play the 2nd string at the third fret.

COOL LICKS: Now go through the tune playing the melody with the drone notes. Next, use the pinch on all the single melody notes.

35

WARM LICKS: Mix up the pinch with the alternating thumb roll on the single melody notes that are on the 3rd or 4th strings (3 2 5 1 or 4 2 5 1).

36

HOT LICKS: On any two melody notes that are next to each other use the reverse roll or the "Foggy Mountain Breakdown" roll.

91/92

RED HOT LICKS: The intro of "When I Lay My Burden Down" is a great place to play a slide. After you hit the 4th string at the second fret, slide up to the fifth fret. This slide will take the place of the first note in measure one. You can follow the slide with either a pinch, an alternating thumb roll (4 3 5 1), or a reverse roll (4 3 1 5 1 2 3 1).

37

Flatt & Scruggs LP

31

Blue Ridge Mountain Blues

This classic has all the ingredients of a great bluegrass song: the Blue Ridge Mountains, leaving and then yearning for home in old Caroline, dogs, aged parents, a light shining through the window, possums, corn, and the moral imperative to "do right." It was first recorded by George Reneau and Gene Austin as "Blue Ridge Blues" in about April of 1924. Not to be outdone, Riley Puckett recorded it on September 10, 1924 as "Blue Ridge Mountain Blues." On May 12, 1927, Al Hopkins & His Buckle Busters recorded a fine version with twin fiddles, which was perhaps the first time twin fiddles were used on a song that would later become a bluegrass classic. The song itself was apparently composed by Cliff Hess in 1924. Little is known about Hess other than the fact that he composed one of the hits of 1917, "Huckleberry Finn." Two years later he wrote or co-wrote "Heart Breaking Baby Doll" and "Freckles."

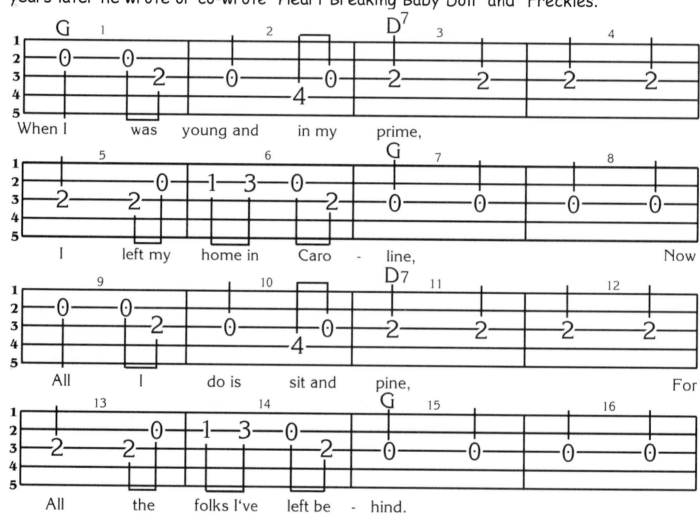

I've got the Blue Ridge Mountain blues
I want to hear those hound dogs bay
I want to hunt the possum
    while the corn tops blossom
In the Blue Ridge far away.

I see a window with a light
I see two heads of snowy white
I seem I hear them both recite
"Where is my wandering boy tonight?"

I'll always do right by my Ma
I'll always do right by my Pa
I'll hang around that cabin door
No work nor worry anymore.

I've got the Blue Ridge Mountain blues
And I stand right here and say
My grip is packed to travel
And I'm scratching gravel
To that Blue Ridge far away.

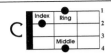
ICE COLD LICKS: Don't be too quick to assume that "Blue Ridge Mountain Blues" is one of those long songs that will take a while to master. In fact, the melody of "Blue Ridge Mountain Blues" is only half as long as it looks because measures 9 - 16 are mirror images of measures 1 - 8. As you're picking out the melody, on measure two be sure to use your ring finger or pinky to play the 4th string at the fourth fret.

COOL LICKS: After you get used to playing the skeleton of the melody, add the drone notes and the pinches on the single melody notes.

WARM LICKS: Since "Blue Ridge Mountain Blues" has so many single melody notes on the 3rd string, it's a perfect song to practice your alternating thumb roll (3 2 5 1). You'll need to play the D7 chord where marked. Mix the alternating thumb roll up with the pinch.

HOT LICKS: You'll notice that the last two measures of each line have four consecutive single melody notes. One way to approach this is on the first two notes you can play with a reverse roll or a "Foggy Mountain Breakdown" roll. On the last two melody notes in each line you can play the pinch.

RED HOT LICKS: In measure one instead of playing the 2nd string open, you can begin the measure with a slide from the 3rd string at the second fret to the 3rd string at the fourth fret. Immediately you can go into a reverse roll (See page 60). The seventh note of the reverse roll will be the 3rd string at the second fret.

Roll in My Sweet Baby's Arms

It was Buster Carter & Preston Young's June 26, 1931 recording that distilled this song into a classic. The Monroe Brothers clearly learned it from this 78 record, and recorded their own version on October 12, 1936. Lester Flatt then learned it from Charlie Monroe when he worked in Charlie's band, the Kentucky Partners. Flatt & Scruggs' killer recording of the song was waxed on October 20, 1950. Flatt & Scruggs must have been impressed with their cut of the song, because they kept it despite a rare mistake when Earl slid up too high and played a sour note. Shame! Shame! Isn't it comforting to know that Earl can mess up too?

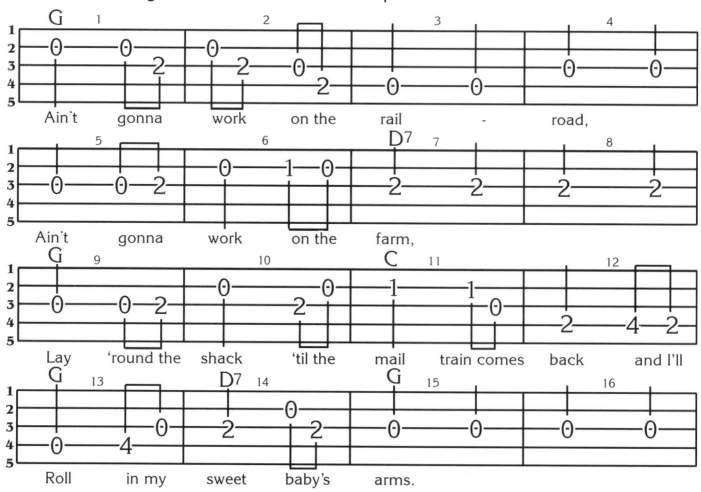

Ain't gonna work on the rail - road,
Ain't gonna work on the farm,
Lay 'round the shack 'til the mail train comes back and I'll
Roll in my sweet baby's arms.

Roll in my sweet baby's arms,
Roll in my sweet baby's arms,
Lay 'round the shack 'til the mail train comes back
And I'll roll in my sweet baby's arms.

Can't see what's a matter with my own true love,
She done quit writing to me,
She must think I don't love her like I used to
Ain't that a foolish idea? [Pronounced "ID"]

Sometimes there's change in the ocean,
Sometimes there's change in the sea
Sometimes there's change in my own true love
But there's never no change in me.

Mama's a ginger cake baker,
Sister can weave and can spin,
Dad's got an interest in that old cotton mill
Just to watch that old money roll in.

They tell me her parents do not like me,
They have drove me away from the door,
If I had all my time to go over
I would never go back any more.

Where were you last Friday night
When I was laying in jail?
Walking the streets with another man
Wouldn't even go my bail.

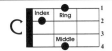

Ice Cold - Red Hot Licks

ICE COLD LICKS: As you play the melody of "Roll in My Sweet Baby's Arms" be sure to use your ring finger or pinky to play the 4th string at the fourth fret on measures twelve and thirteen.

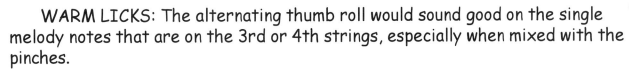

COOL LICKS: Now add the drone notes and pinches on the single melody notes.

WARM LICKS: The alternating thumb roll would sound good on the single melody notes that are on the 3rd or 4th strings, especially when mixed with the pinches.

HOT LICKS: Let's try using the forward roll in measure one. Starting either with your right index finger or thumb, your roll would go 2 1 5 2 1 5 3 1. Of course, when you hit the 3rd string you'll be fretting it at the second fret. You can also play the forward roll on measure five and nine by playing 3 1 5 3 1 5 3 1. This time, when you hit the last 3rd string, you'll need to fret the 3rd string at the second fret. If you want to continue with the forward roll on measure six, you'd start the forward roll with 2 1 5. Then fret the 2nd string at the first fret and play 2 1 5. Next, take your finger off the 2nd string at the first fret, and finish your forward roll with 2 1. The entire forward roll would be:

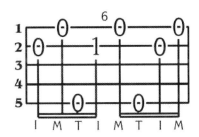

RED HOT LICKS: On measures three, seven, and fifteen you can play the reverse roll or the "Foggy Mountain Breakdown" roll.

Wabash Cannonball

Alan Lomax said it best when he described the mythical train known as the Wabash Cannonball: "Each tie was made from an entire redwood tree. The conductor punched each ticket by shooting holes through it with a .45 caliber automatic. The train went so fast that after it was brought to a dead stop, it was still making sixty-five miles an hour." The song was first printed in 1904, but was based on an earlier song by the name of "The Great Rock Island Route" by J.A. Roff, published in 1882.

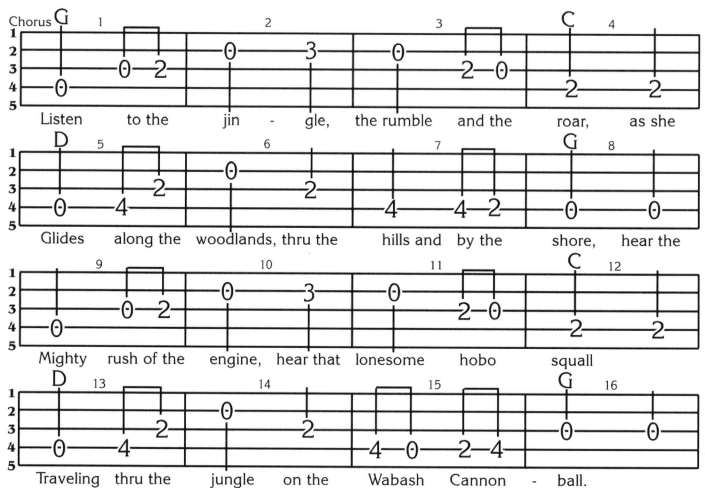

From the great Atlantic ocean to the wide Pacific shore,
From the queen of flowing mountains to the south bells by the shore,
She's mighty tall and handsome and quite well known by all,
She's the combination of the Wabash Cannonball. (Chorus)

She come down from Birmingham one cold December day,
And she rolled into the station you could hear the people say,
There's a girl from Birmingham, she's long and she is tall,
She come down from Birmingham on the Wabash Cannonball. (Chorus)

Here's to Daddy Claxton, may his name forever stand,
And always be remembered in the courts of Alabam,
His earth race is over and the curtains round him fall,
We'll carry him home to victory on the Wabash Cannonball. (Chorus)

ICE COLD LICKS: As usual, first you'll want to play the bare melody with your thumb. On measure five you'll need to go to a D chord (page 62). Here, I'd make a two-finger D chord by fretting the 3rd string at the second fret and the 2nd string at the third fret. After playing the 4th string open, you'll need to fret the 4th string at the fourth fret with your ring finger or pinky. Next, you'll play the 3rd string at the second fret, but, thanks to the fact that you began measure five by fretting the D chord, you've already got the 3rd string at the second fret covered! Even though you'll need to lift up your index finger to play the 2nd string open in measure six, you should leave your index finger where it is, so you can play the 3rd string at the second fret.

45

COOL LICKS: Play "Wabash Cannonball" using your drone notes and pinches.

46

WARM LICKS: When the melody falls on the 2nd string, you can substitute the two-finger roll for the pinch (2 1 5 1). On the single melody notes, mix up your pinches with the alternating thumb roll (3 2 5 1 or 4 2 5 1).

47

HOT LICKS: Instead of playing the 2nd string open in measure two, you can do a slide in combination with an alternating thumb roll. After you hit the second fret note in the first measure, slide up on the 3rd string to the fourth fret quickly followed by the rest of the alternating thumb roll.

95

RED HOT LICKS: On the last measure of each line you can play a reverse roll if you like.

91

Red River Valley

This well-known campfire favorite makes a dandy bluegrass banjo piece. Who knew?

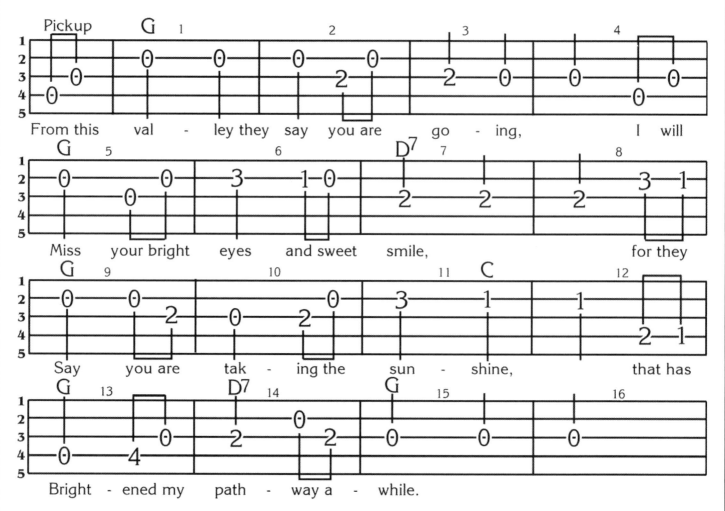

From this val - ley they say you are go - ing, I will
Miss your bright eyes and sweet smile, for they
Say you are tak - ing the sun - shine, that has
Bright - ened my path - way a - while.

Chorus:
    Come and sit by my side if you love me.
    Do not hasten to bid me adieu.
    But remember the Red River Valley
    And the cowboy who loved you so true.

I've been waiting a long time my darling
For the sweet words you never would say.
Now at last all my fond hopes have vanished,
For they say you are going away. (Chorus)

O there never could be such a longing
In the heart of a poor cowboy's breast.
That now dwells in the heart you are breaking,
As I wait in my home in the West. (Chorus)

Do you think of the valley you're leaving?
O how lonely and drear it will be!
Do you think of the kind heart you're breaking,
And the pain you are causing to me? (Chorus)

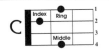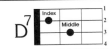

ICE COLD LICKS: As you pick out the melody of this old cowboy song, notice measures three and eleven. On both of these measures, the notes are usually sung quicker than they are shown here. For ease of playing with blue-grass rolls, I've spaced out the notes. If you listen to the recording, you'll understand this better.

48

COOL LICKS: After you've got a handle on playing the melody of "Red River Valley," play it with drone notes and pinches.

49

WARM LICKS: In place of the pinch, use the alternating thumb roll on any single melody notes that are on the 3rd or 4th strings (3 2 5 1 or 4 2 5 1).

HOT LICKS: Take a peek at measures one and two and you'll see that the 2nd is played open three times. Instead of playing those as written, I'd be tempted to play three slides, each with an alternating thumb roll. Right after the pickup, fret the 3rd string at the second fret and slide up to the fourth fret. As you start your slide, play the rest of your alternating thumb roll (2 5 1). Play the slide with the alternating thumb roll a total of three times in place of the 2nd string open in measures one and two.

50

RED HOT LICKS: On measure twelve, you might want to try playing part of a forward roll. To do this, notice that you're still holding down your C chord from measure eleven. Begin measure twelve by playing 5 2 1 5. If you decide to try this, keep in mind that since you just used your thumb to play the last 5, you'll need to play the 4th string at the second and first frets with your right index finger. On track 51 of the recording I'm playing measures eleven and twelve.

51

Little Maggie

Bluegrass musicians have always had a soft spot in their hearts for songs about hard drinking and wild women. No wonder that "Little Maggie" remains a favorite. It was first recorded by Henry Whitter and G.B. Grayson on August 1, 1928. Next to record it was Wade Mainer and Zeke Morris on August 2, 1937. The theme of the song, and at least one of the verses, is shared with the song "Darlin' Corey."

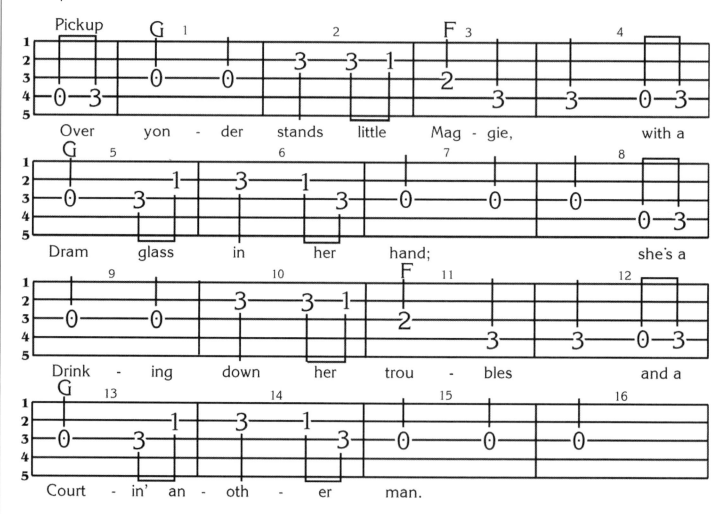

Oh how can I ever stand it
To see those two blue eyes;
They're shining in the moonlight
Like two diamonds in the sky.

Pretty flowers were made for blooming
Pretty stars were made to shine;
Pretty women were made for loving
Little Maggie was made for mine.

Oh, the last time I saw little Maggie,
She was sitting on the banks of the sea.
With her forty-four strapped around her
And a banjo on her knee.

I'm going down to the station
With my suitcase in my hand;
I'm going to leave this country
I'm going to some far and distant land.

Go 'way, go 'way little Maggie,
Go and do the best you can.
I'll get me another woman
You can get you another man.

Ice Cold - Red Hot Licks

ICE COLD LICKS: The melody of "Little Maggie" has kind of a minor flavor and you'll see that both the 3rd and 4th strings are fretted at the third fret. Be sure to use your ring finger on the 2nd string at the third fret so you'll barely have to move your hand to play the 2nd string at the first fret. On measure three you don't have to make a complete F chord. Just fret the 3rd string at the second fret and the 4th string at the third fret. Keep in mind that "Little Maggie" is not as long as it looks. The song basically repeats starting with the last two notes of measure eight.

CHORDS: At this point you don't need to bother to play the F chord in "Little Maggie," and it sounds fine without it.

COOL LICKS: After you get the melody of "Little Maggie" down pat, add your drone notes and pinches.

WARM LICKS: I would NOT play the alternating thumb roll on "Little Maggie." To preserve the minor flavor of the song, you want to avoid playing the 2nd string open.

HOT LICKS: "Little Maggie" is a great song to use your forward roll and mixing it up with the "Foggy Mountain Breakdown" roll. On the recording, I play the forward roll on measures one and seven and the "Foggy Mountain Break-down" roll on measures nine and fifteen.

Wade Mainer, 1940s

Long Journey Home

Originating as far back as 1890, "Long Journey Home" was earlier known as "High Sheriff" and "Deadheads and Suckers." In their first recording session on February 27, 1936, the Monroe Brothers chose "Long Journey Home" as the first song they recorded.

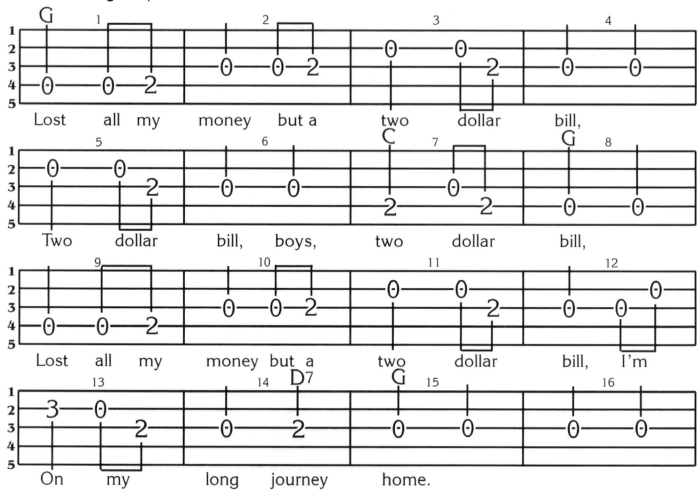

Black smoke's a rising, surely it's a train,
Surely it's a train, boys, surely it's a train.
Black smoke's a rising, surely it's a train,
I'm on my long journey home.

Homesick and lonesome and feeling kinda blue,
Feeling kinda blue, boys, feeling kinda blue.
Homesick and lonesome and feeling kinda blue,
I'm on my long journey home.

Dark and a-raining and I got to go home,
Got to go home, boys, got to go home.
Dark and a-raining and I got to go home,
I'm on my long journey home.

ICE COLD LICKS: As you play just the melody of "Long Journey Home" with your thumb, you can quickly see that all the notes are all easy to find. Happily, line one and line three are the same.

COOL LICKS: Now play the song with your drone notes and pinches.

WARM LICKS: When you're comfortable with the tune, add the alternating thumb roll (3 2 5 1 or 4 2 5 1) and mix it in with the pinches.

HOT LICKS: The melody of "Long Journey Home" is actually quite plain, so it's good to think of a few things to perk it up. The first thing to try are slides. As you'll soon see, the placement of the melody makes this song an ideal place to use slides. Take measure one, for example. If you slide the second fret note up to the fifth fret, you get the same note as the 3rd string open, which begins measure two. On the slide you can use an alternating thumb roll if you like (3 2 5 1). On the recording I'll play measure one and the first half of measure two.

At the risk of overdoing it, on measure two you can slide again from the second fret on the 3rd string up to the fourth fret, followed by the alternating thumb roll. Since line three is identical to line one, you can do the same thing on line three as you did on line one.

My Home's Across the Blue Ridge Mountains

Louise Rand Bascom first collected a fragment of this song in North Carolina under the title "My Own True Love" in 1909 for an article for the *Journal of American Folklore*. Bascom Lamar Lunsford learned this song about the same time, but called it "My Home's Across the Smoky Mountains." It was first recorded as "I'm Going Back to North Carolina" by Kelly Harrell in Asheville, North Carolina in August of 1925. The first to call it "My Home's Across the Blue Ridge Mountains" was apparently the Carolina Tar Heels, who recorded it in Camden, New Jersey on April 3, 1929.

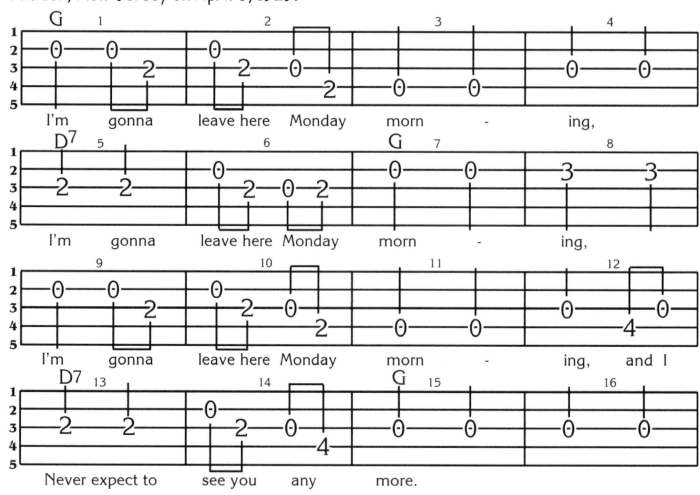

My home's across the Blue Ridge Mountains,
My home's across the Blue Ridge Mountains,
My home's across the Blue Ridge Mountains,
And I never expect to see you anymore.

How can I keep from cryin'
How can I keep from cryin'
How can I keep from cryin'
And I never expect to see you anymore.

Rock and feed my baby candy,
Rock and feed my baby candy,
Rock and feed my baby candy,
And I never expect to see you anymore.

So goodbye my Asheville darling,
So goodbye my Asheville darling,
So goodbye my Asheville darling,
And I never expect to see you anymore.

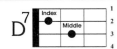

Ice Cold - Red Hot Licks

59

ICE COLD LICKS: The melody of "My Home's Across the Blue Ridge Mountains" is quite straightforward, so it should be pretty easy to play. Make sure to use your ring finger or pinky in measures twelve and fourteen on the fourth fret notes.

COOL LICKS: This time, play the tune with the drone notes and pinches.

60

WARM LICKS: You can warm up the song with the alternating thumb roll on any of the single melody notes you find on the 3rd or 4th string (3 2 5 1 or 4 2 5 1). Mix it in with the pinches.

61

HOT LICKS: "My Home's Across the Blue Ridge Mountains" is a good song to strut your reverse roll. I would suggest you try it on measure three. Although you could also play it on measure four, that might be overdoing it, so I'd play pinches on measure four. Then you can come back in the reverse roll in measure five. You can also play the reverse roll in measures eleven, thirteen and fifteen.

RED HOT LICKS: You can add some variety to the song by playing a forward roll in measure seven. In this case, I'd start with my thumb. Here is the forward roll:

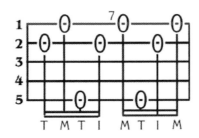

89

Notice above that I left off the last note, so it is just a seven note roll.

Now it's time to play "My Home's Across the Blue Ridge Mountains" with all the rolls we've tried so far with this song: pinch, alternating thumb roll, reverse roll and forward roll.

62

Pass Me Not

It was in 1868 that Dr. William H. Doane asked Fanny J. Crosby to write a hymn on the theme "Pass me not, O gentle Savior." Blinded by an accident in early childhood, Crosby was a gifted composer and poet who was said to have written over 8,000 poems. Her composition of "Pass Me Not" was set to music by Doane and first published in his *Songs of Devotion* in 1870. It was popularized by Ira D. Sankey at the revivals held by evangelist Dwight L. Moody.

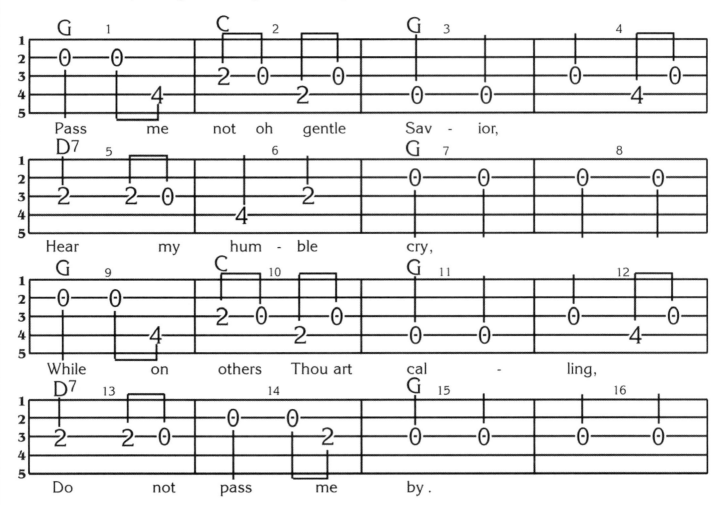

Chorus:

   G   C
   Savior, Savior,
   G   D7
   Hear my humble cry,
   G   C   G
   While on others you are calling,
   D7   G
   Do not pass me by.

Let me at a throne of mercy,
Find a sweet relief,
Kneeling there in deep contrition,
Hear my unbelief. (Chorus)

Trusting only in Thy merit,
Would I seek Thy face?
Heal my wounded, broken spirit,
Save me by Thy grace. (Chorus)

Though the spring of all my comfort,
More than life to me,
Whom have I on earth beside Thee
Whom in heaven but Thee? (Chorus)

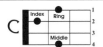 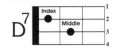
ICE COLD LICKS: The quirky melody of "Pass Me Not" means we have to pay particular attention to left hand fingerings. On measure one, you would use your ring finger or pinky to play the fourth fret note. After that you have to race to get to the second fret note at the beginning of measure two. You should position your hand so your index finger is close to that note just before it's time to hit it. That way, you won't have to stop playing to get to that note.

COOL LICKS: When adding drone notes, I would avoid the drone notes between the notes that are hard to get to. A good drone note to leave out would be right after the fourth fret note in measure one. Add your pinches.

WARM LICKS: If you want to kick off the song off with a bang, you can start out with a slide. Instead of playing the 2nd string open at the beginning of measure one, simply slide on the 3rd string from the second to the fourth fret. Quickly follow that with a pinch or alternating thumb roll. On the recording I'll play measure one with the alternating thumb roll.

HOT LICKS: Measures three, eleven and fifteen would be likely places to play a reverse roll (4 2 1 5 1 2 3 1 or 3 2 1 5 1 2 3 1). Of course, the last note of this roll is optional.

RED HOT LICKS: Measures seven and eight are just crying for some kind of embellishment. On those measures I'd be tempted to substitute the 2nd string played open with a slide from the 3rd string at the second fret to the fourth fret. I would then do an alternating thumb roll four times, each preceded by a slide.

Pretty Polly

The cruel murder of Pretty Polly was at the hands of a ship's carpenter named John Billson near Gosport, England. The ballad was first printed in about 1727 as "The Gosport Tragedy," and sung to the tune of "Peggy's Gone Over Sea." Legends tell that Polly avenged her own murder by coming back to haunt her murderer.

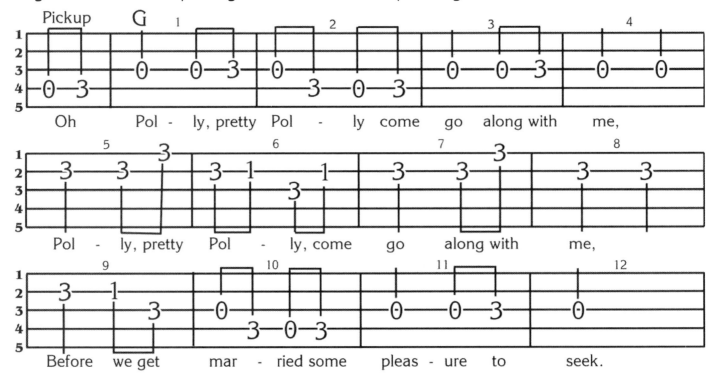

Where is Pretty Polly, oh yonder she stands (2X)
Gold rings on her fingers and her lily white hands.

I led her over hills and valleys so deep (2X)
And then Pretty Polly she began to weep.

Willie, oh Willie, I'm afraid of your ways (2X)
I'm afraid you are going for to lead me astray.

Polly, Pretty Polly, your guess is about right, (2X)
I dug on your grave the biggest part of last night.

We went a little further and what did she spy (2X)
A new dug grave with a spade lying by.

She threw her arms around me and begged for her life (2X)
So deep into her bosom I plunged the fatal knife.

She fell to the ground and the blood it did flow (2X)
And then to her grave pretty Polly did go.

I threw the dirt around her and turned to go home (2X)
And left Pretty Polly for the birds to weep and mourn.

Now to the devil the debt I must pay (2X)
For killing Pretty Polly and running away.

Ice Cold - Red Hot Licks

ICE COLD LICKS: The spooky melody of "Pretty Polly" will be fun to pick out. You'll find many of the melody notes on the third fret of the 1st, 3rd and 4th strings. Be sure to use your ring finger on all the notes on the third fret.

COOL LICKS: Add the drone notes and pinches to the melody. It's not necessary to play drone notes after the 3rd fret notes that are tied together in measures five or seven.

WARM LICKS: The thing that makes "Pretty Polly" sound so haunting is that the song is set in kind of a minor key. What this means for you is that for this song, you should NOT hit the 2nd string open or unfretted, so you can't use your alternating thumb roll. Luckily, there's a way around this. Fret the 2nd string at the first fret. Now play the alternating thumb roll starting on the 3rd string (3 2 5 1). That's the sound you want. If it doesn't sound quite right, it may be that you just have to get used to this eerie sound. So on any of the single melody notes that are the 3rd string open, fret the 2nd string at the first fret and try your alternating thumb roll. Of course, you can also mix the alternating thumb roll in with the pinches.

HOT LICKS: The stark melody of "Pretty Polly" is best played simply, without too many hot licks, so let's stick with the pinch and alternating thumb roll.

49

Put My Little Shoes Away

Parlors of the late 19th century were often filled with songs that were dripping with sentimentality. Long after these kinds of songs were pushed aside to make way for the more upbeat songs of a new century, they were treasured by rural people who relished a good cry. "Put My Little Shoes Away" was published in Boston in 1873, with lyrics by Samuel N. Mitchell and music by Charles E. Pratt.

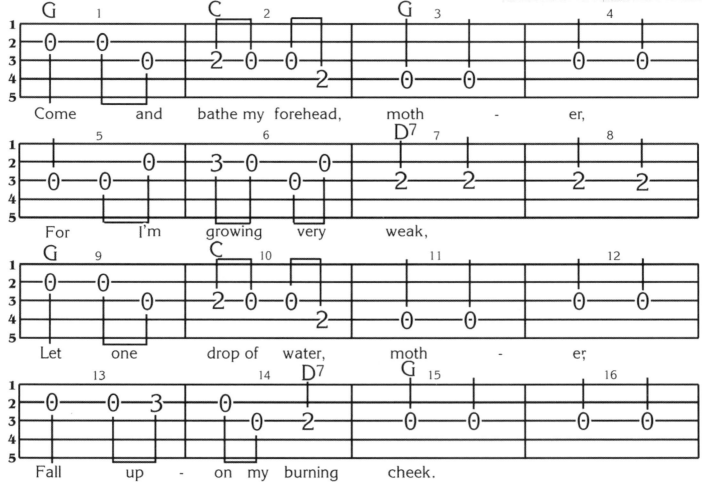

Come and bathe my forehead, moth - er,

For I'm growing very weak,

Let one drop of water, moth - er,

Fall up - on my burning cheek.

C   G
You will do this won't you mother?
         D7
Please remember what I say
G   C   G
Give them all my toys but mother,
   D7   G
Put my little shoes away.

Tell my loving little playmates
That I nevermore will play;
Give them all my toys but mother,
Put my little shoes away. (Chorus)

Santa Claus, he brought them to me
With a lot of other things;
And I think he brought an angel
With a pair of golden wings. (Chorus)

Soon the baby will grow larger
Then they'll fit his little feet;
Oh! he'll look so nice and cunning
When he walks along the street. (Chorus)

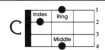
ICE COLD LICKS: Pick out the melody to start things off.

COOL LICKS: Throw in your drone notes and pinches.

WARM LICKS: On the last two measures of all four lines you can play the alternating thumb roll on all the single melody notes. Mix it up with the pinches.

HOT LICKS: Haul out your reverse roll and use it on measures three, seven, eleven and fifteen. After you play the reverse roll on those measures, play the pinch on the next measure.

RED HOT LICKS: Let's incorporate the forward roll into measure one of "Put My Little Shoes Away." In this case you would play 2 1 5 2 1 5 3 1. You can play the first note of this roll either with your index finger or thumb.

You can also play the forward roll in measure five. Here you would play 3 1 5 3 1 5 2 1.

Since measures 1-4 are identical to measures 9-12, you can play the forward roll in measure nine just as we did in measure one.

Measure thirteen is another place you can strut your forward roll. As you can see, the melody is entirely on the 2nd string. On the final melody note, you would of course fret the 2nd string at the third fret. The roll itself would go 2 1 5 2 1 5 2 1. You'll probably want to leave off the last note of the roll to give you some breathing room before you start in on measure fourteen.

Shall We Gather at the River

This popular hymn was written in 1865 by Robert Lowry and first recorded by the Alcoa Quartet on January 29, 1925. Next to record it on May 10, 1927 was Uncle Dave Macon and Sam and Kirk McGee, who billed themselves as the Dixie Sacred Singers. By the way, it was one of Uncle Dave Macon's favorite hymns.

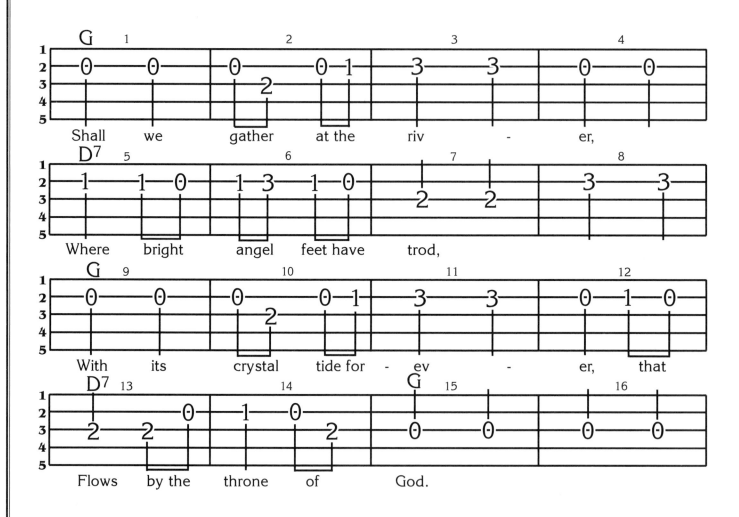

Chorus:

C   G
Yes, we'll gather at the river,

      D7   G
The beautiful, the beautiful river,

C   G
Gather with the saints at the river,

      D7   G
That flows by the throne of God.

On the margin of the river,
Washing up its silver spray,
We will walk and worship ever
All the happy golden day. (Chorus)

There we reach the shining river,
Lay we every burden down,
Grace our spirits will deliver,
And provide a robe and crown. (Chorus)

Soon we'll reach the shining river,
Soon our pilgrimage will cease,
Soon our happy hearts will quiver,
With the melody of peace. (Chorus)

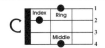 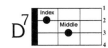
ICE COLD LICKS: As you leap into the melody of "Shall We Gather at the River," keep in mind that you'll find all the notes on the first three frets. As usual, use your index finger on the first fret, your middle finger on the second fret, and your ring finger on the third fret.

COOL LICKS: Throw in your drone notes and pinches.

73

WARM LICKS: There's not much room for the alternating thumb roll, but you can use it on measures seven, thirteen, fifteen and sixteen. You can mix the alternating roll in with the pinch.

HOT LICKS: Now let's use the forward roll on measure one. Since the melody is entirely on the 2nd string, we can simply play 2 1 5 2 1 5 2 1.

Looking further on down line one of "Shall We Gather at the River," we can also play the forward roll on measure three. You can also use it on measure four, but for variety you might want to use pinches here.

Measure five is an interesting place to use a forward roll. Simply fret the 2nd string at the first fret and play 2 1 5 2 1 5 2 1. Of course, the last time you play the 2nd string, you would take your finger off of the first fret and play it open.

74

Since line three is almost the same as line one, you can use the forward roll in all the same places as you did there.

RED HOT LICKS: To add a little spice, you can use the "Foggy Mountain Breakdown" roll on measures one, three, seven, eleven, and/or fifteen.

On the recording, I'll play the forward roll on measures one, three, five, nine, and eleven and the "Foggy Mountain Breakdown" roll on measures seven and fifteen.

75

Note: On the chorus, you can just keep the rhythm with your rolls while changing chords.

When the Saints Go Marching In

Evidence of the origin of this Negro spiritual points to the Bahama Islands, but we may never know the truth. It was first copyrighted on June 17, 1896 by J. M. Black, who wrote "*When the Roll is Called Up Yonder*" in 1898. It appeared in Black's book, *Songs for the Soul No. 2* with music by J. M. Black and lyrics by Katherine E. Purvis. It is quite possible that Black and Purvis merely "arranged" it. Now, it's our turn to *arrange* it for bluegrass banjo.

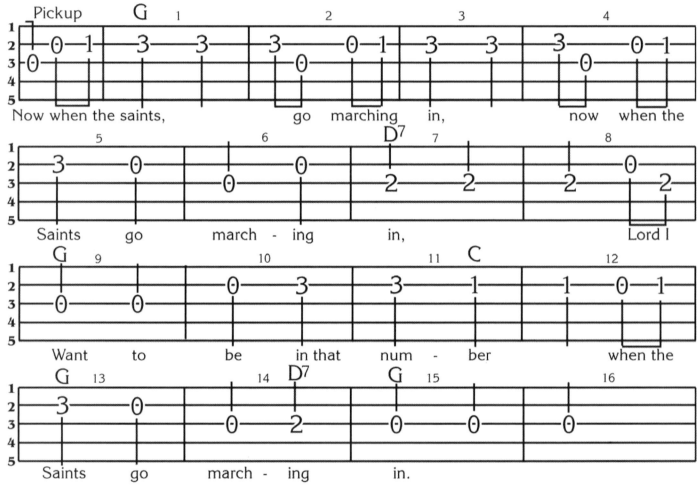

And when the sun refuse to shine,
When the sun refuse to shine,
Oh Lord I want to be in that number
When the sun refuse to shine.

Oh when the trumpet sounds its call,
When the trumpet sounds its call,
Oh Lord I want to be in that number
When the trumpet sounds its call.

And when they crown him Lord of all,
When they crown him Lord of all,
Oh Lord I want to be in that number,
When they crown him Lord of all.

 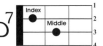

ICE COLD LICKS: As you play the melody of "When the Saints Go Marching In" you may notice a few quirky things. First off, the intro has three pick-up notes instead of our normal two. No big deal.

COOL LICKS: Go through and play your drone notes and pinches. It's probably a good idea to omit drone notes on the end of any measure so you'll have a moment to think before the next measure.

WARM LICKS: You can play the alternating thumb roll and/or pinch on measures seven, nine, fourteen, fifteen and sixteen.

HOT LICKS: "When the Saints Go Marching In" was practically written for the forward roll. It fits easily in measures one and three without much fuss. On measure five, you can again use the forward roll, but be sure to fret the 2nd string at the third fret through the first six notes of your roll and then play the open 2nd string. It would look like this:

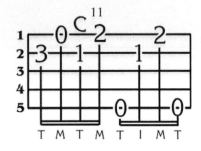

RED HOT LICKS: On measure seven, you can use your "Foggy Mountain Breakdown" roll if you feel so inclined.

While you've got your "Foggy Mountain Breakdown" roll dusted off, you can also use it to play measure eleven, which is kind of a goofy measure in itself. I would suggest you start the measure by fretting the 2nd string at the third fret and play the first two notes of "Foggy Mountain Breakdown" roll and then switch to a C chord to finish the roll. In this case, I would use my thumb the first two times you play the 2nd string. Here it is:

On the recording, I'm playing the forward roll on measures, one, three, five, nine and thirteen, and the "Foggy Mountain Breakdown" roll on measures seven, eleven and fifteen.

55

Man of Constant Sorrow

Kentucky-born blind street singer Dick Burnett had every reason to write "I am a Man of Constant Sorrow." An orphan by the time he was twelve, Burnett was almost murdered in 1907 when he was robbed and shot in the face with a shotgun. Suddenly blinded, Burnett took to playing on the streets to help support his wife and his child. He composed this song in about 1912. These are the original lyrics as first recorded by Emry Arthur on January 1, 1928.

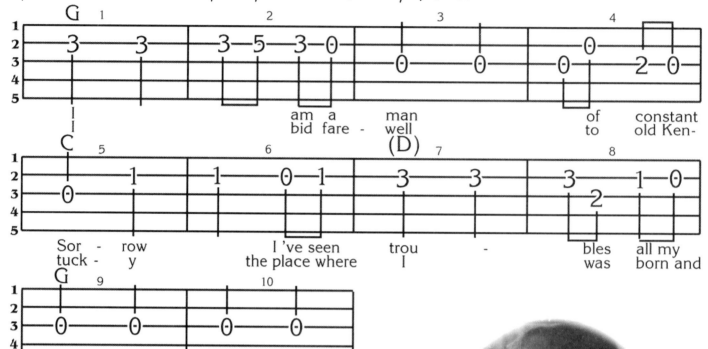

Days.
Raised.

For six long years I've been in trouble
My pleasure here on earth is done.
For in this world I have to ramble,
I have no friends to help me now.

Oh, fare you well my own true lover,
I fear I'll never see you again.
For I am bound to ride the northern railroad,
Perhaps I'll die upon the train.

Oh, you can bury me in some deep valley,
For many years there I may lay.
And while you're dreaming while you're slumbering
While I am sleeping in the grave.

Oh its fare thee well to my native country,
The place where I have loved so well.
For I have had all kinds of trouble,
In this vain world no tongue can tell.

But friends all know I may be a stranger,
My face you may never see no more.
But there's one promise that's been given,
Where we can meet on the beautiful shore.

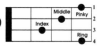

ICE COLD LICKS: As you play the melody of "Man of Constant Sorrow" you'll want to think ahead so you can use the proper fingers of your left hand. Starting with the first measure, use your left index finger to fret the third fret notes. On measure two you'll need to reach up and play the fifth fret note with your ring finger or pinky. Looking at measure eight, you'll notice that you'll be playing in the first three frets, so you'll want to use your first three fingers. Your ring finger should play the third fret note, your middle finger should fret the second fret note and your index finger will play the first fret note.

COOL LICKS: Add drone notes on measures two, four, six and eight. Don't forget you can omit the last drone note in a measure to give you breathing room. Put in your pinches after each single melody note.

WARM LICKS: Go through "Man of Constant Sorrow" using the alternating thumb roll after each single melody note that's on the 3rd string. You'll find those in measures three, five, nine and ten. Mix in some pinches.

CHORDS: After playing the tune several times using the alternative thumb roll and the drone notes, add the chords. Notice measure seven calls for a D chord. It's shown in parentheses because the D chord is optional. If you'd like to try it, simply add the 1st string at the fourth fret while you're fretting the 2nd string at the third fret. It may sound "off" or wrong to you at first. Just think about it like you would adding chile powder to a bland dish. It'll give the tune some spice.

HOT LICKS: Let's dress up the tune from the git-go by adding a slide on the first third fret in measure one. (See page 61 on the slide). With your left index finger, fret the 2nd string at the first fret. Hit the 2nd string with your right thumb or index finger and then immediately slide your index finger up to the third fret. On the recording I'm just playing the slide followed by a pinch.

RED HOT LICKS: Whether or not you use a slide in measure one, those third fret notes on the 2nd string are simply begging for a forward roll. While fretting the 2nd string at the third fret, play 2 1 5 2 1 5 2 1. You can also play the forward roll in measures three, seven and nine. If you play the D chord it will sound WICKED!

WHITE HOT LICKS: This is a good tune to use your "Foggy Mountain Breakdown" roll. Begin measure one with a slide and go right into the "Foggy Mountain Breakdown" roll. Your notes would be 2 1 2 1 5 2 1 5. You can do the same thing on measure seven, combining it with the D chord. When you play measures three, nine and ten, you can also play the "Foggy Mountain Breakdown" roll. Here you would play 3 1 3 1 5 3 1 5. Note that if you use the roll too much it will sound repetitive. If you play it on measure nine, for example, I'd use a pinch on measure ten.

Beginning Rolls

PINCH: The pinch is the easiest and most versatile roll. You start it by playing a melody note with your thumb on the 2nd, 3rd, or 4th string. Then you pluck or "pinch" the 1st and 5th strings at the same time using your middle finger and thumb. It's important to use your middle finger on the 1st string. On any of the songs in this book, when you see one or two single melody notes by themselves in a measure, you can play the pinch right after each note.

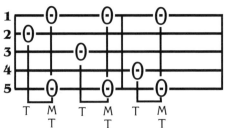

TWO-FINGER ROLL: Here is another versatile roll that you can substitute for, or alternate with, the pinch. Like the pinch, you can use the two-finger roll any time you find a single melody note in the tablature by itself on the 2nd, 3rd or 4th string. You'll basically be playing 2 1 5 1 or 3 1 5 1 or 4 1 5 1. The first of these four notes is your melody note.

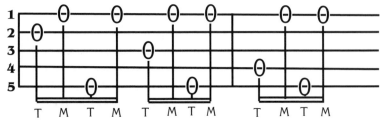

PEGLEG SAILOR ROLL: This is merely a variation of the two-finger roll. Merely leave off the second note of the two-finger roll, so you're playing 2 _ 5 1 or 3 _ 5 1 or 4 _ 5 1. The second note, which you're not playing, has the same timing as the other three notes. By the way, I call this the pegleg sailor roll because this lopsided roll makes me think of a pegleg sailor hobbling down the dock.

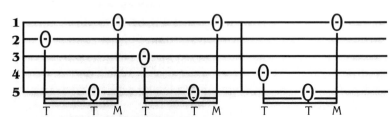

ALTERNATING THUMB ROLL: This essential roll has the same timing as the two-finger roll, except that at last we'll be using three fingers: thumb (T), index (I) and middle (M). Although an essential roll in bluegrass banjo picking, it is not as versatile as the pinch or two-finger roll because you can only use it when the melody is on the 3rd or 4th strings. You can either play 3 2 5 1 or 4 2 5 1.

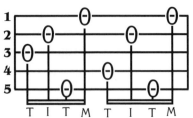

Forward Roll

FORWARD ROLL: This will be our first eight-note roll, and one of the most challenging to master. You WILL get the hang of it, so hang in there! By definition, a forward roll is a roll where your fingers move in a clockwise direction. Hold your hand in front of your face with the palm of your hand facing away from you. If you start the forward roll with your index finger, the next finger in a clockwise direction would be your middle finger and then your thumb, and so on. Before you try incorporating the forward roll into your songs, be sure that you've already played through all the songs using the pinch, two-finger roll and the alternating thumb roll. Only then will you be ready to work on the forward roll.

When the melody is on the 2nd string, your forward roll would go 2 1 5 2 1 5 2 1. Be sure to use your index finger on all the second fret notes. When the melody is on the 3rd string, you would play the forward roll 3 1 5 3 1 5 3 1. Again, use your index finger on all the third fret notes. When the melody is on the 4th string, you would play 4 1 5 4 1 5 4 1 using your index finger on the fourth fret notes. Here is the forward roll in tablature. Measure one has the melody on the 2nd string, measure two has the melody on the 3rd string and measure three has it on the 4th string.

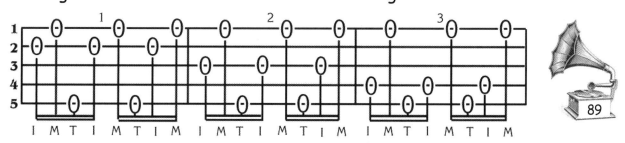

Depending on the melody of the song, the first, fourth and seventh note of the roll can be on the 2nd, 3rd, or 4th strings. For practice, start your forward roll with 2 1 5 2 1 5 2 1, and then try 2 1 5 3 1 5 2 1 or 3 1 5 2 1 5 3 1 or 4 1 5 3 1 5 2 1 or any of the other combinations possible. Practice keeping the forward roll going while you switch strings in a variety of combinations.

After you've gotten the forward roll down cold starting with your index finger, you can also use your thumb at the beginning of the roll. The other fingers will stay the same. How do you know whether to use your index finger or thumb in a song? A lot depends on what you just played. If you just finished using your thumb, perhaps you'd prefer using your index finger to start off the forward roll. I generally find on fast songs, I like using my index finger to lead with on the forward roll. Where accuracy is more important than speed, I often favor my thumb to begin the forward roll. It's also easier to emphasize the melody using the thumb. Your goal should be to be able to use either your thumb or your index finger on any given forward roll. That way, you'll be the most versatile.

Note: You can leave off the last or eighth note of the forward roll any time you want. Leaving it off gives you a nice little space before the start of the next roll. To add interest, you can occasionally leave off the second note of the forward roll.

More Rolls

REVERSE ROLL: This roll is sometimes called the backward roll or the forward/reverse roll. It starts with your fingers moving in a forward or clockwise direction, and then it reverses direction so your fingers move in a counterclockwise direction. It sounds trickier than it is. The reverse roll is limited to playing the melody on the 3rd, 4th or 5th strings. You can play either 3 2 1 5 1 2 3 1 or 4 2 1 5 1 2 3 1 or 5 2 1 5 1 2 3 1. Like the forward roll, the last note is completely optional and can certainly be left off. The seventh note can be played as a 3, or a 4, depending on the melody of the tune.

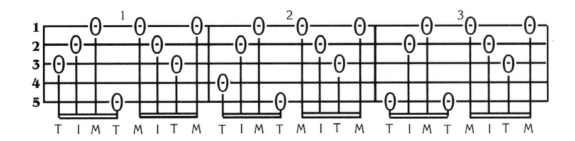

"FOGGY MOUNTAIN BREAKDOWN" ROLL is named after the tune by Earl Scruggs that uses this roll so prominently. Starting with your index finger, it goes 2 1 2 1 5 2 1 5. On the second 2 you would use your thumb but on the last 2 you would use your index finger. I addition to starting on the 2nd string, you can also begin the roll with the 3rd string: 3 1 3 1 5 3 1 5. On the sixth note of the roll you can play either a 2, a 3, or even a 4. When you start this roll with the 3rd string you can begin the roll with your thumb if you like. In this case, you would be playing thumb middle, thumb middle and then the rest of the roll. If you play it over and over, you can only use your thumb the first time you play it. This is because the roll ends with the thumb. You certainly wouldn't want to play your thumb twice in a row, now would you?

Earl Scruggs

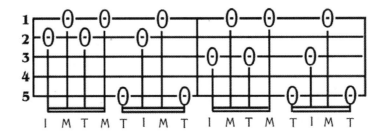

Slides

3RD STRING SLIDES. Slides are an essential tool in bluegrass banjo pickin' and are very fun to do. Fret the 3rd string at the second fret with your left middle finger. Strike the string with your right thumb and quickly slide your middle finger up to the fourth fret. The idea is to keep enough pressure on the string as you slide so the note will still be ringing when you get to the fourth fret.

Immediately after the slide on the 3rd string from the second to the fourth frets, you can play a pinch .

Instead of the pinch, after you do the 3rd string slide you can play the alternating thumb roll.

Note: The slide on the 3rd string from the second to the fourth fret can be substituted for any single melody note in this book that is on the 2nd string played open or unfretted. Take the "Bile 'Em Cabbage Down," for example, on page 14. You could play the slide with a pinch or alternating thumb roll on either or both notes in measures one, three or five.

In addition to using the pinch and the alternating thumb on the 3rd string slide, you can also use the reverse roll: 3 2 1 5 1 2 3 1.

4TH STRING SLIDES. A slide can also be used on the 4th string. Merely fret the 4th string at the second fret with your middle finger and slide up to the fifth fret. You can then play a pinch.

If you want to use your alternating thumb roll while doing the fourth string slide, you have to change the strings you usually play on the alternating thumb roll to 4 3 5 1.

Banjo Chords

Unlike the guitar, most chords on a banjo are painfully easy. You'll find that the average bluegrass song uses only three chords: G, C and D7. Since your banjo is tuned to a G chord you don't even have to put the fingers of your left hand on the strings to play the G. What could be easier?

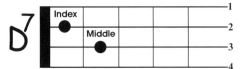

For the C, put your left index finger on the 2nd string at the first fret, your middle finger on the 4th string at the second fret and your ring finger at the 1st string at the second fret. It is essential that you place your fingers down on the strings at the same time. Note: It's rare that you'll be playing the 4th string while on the C chord, so a two-finger C chord will work 98% of the time. Be sure to use your ring finger on the 1st string, so when you do need to play the 4th string while on a C you'll have your middle available to pounce on that string.

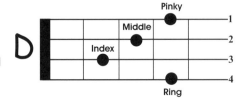

To play a D7, put your left index finger on the 2nd string at the first fret and your middle finger on the 3rd string at the second fret. Just like I said on the C chord above, it is very important that you place BOTH of your fingers down on the strings at the same time. Trust me. This will make a big difference in the time it takes you to make a chord.

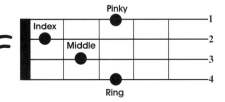

I usually play a D7 instead of a D, but there will be times when a D chord will be useful. You can make the D chord several ways. The easiest way is just to play a two-finger D, using your index and middle fingers. For spice, you can add the pinky. On rare occasions you'll need the ring finger on the 4th string.

Although you won't need F very often, on songs like "Little Maggie," it is essential. It's fingered similar to a D7, except with more fingers. Sometimes on the F you won't be playing the 4th string, so when that happens, you can leave it off.

Note to ignoramuses: If you are a certified ignoramus and you're just playing the ice cold and the cool licks, you can ignore the chords that are written above each song in the book. When you advance to the warmer licks, you can begin to add the chords if you like, but most of the songs will sound fine if you continue to ignore the chords. Add the chords only if you think it makes a song sound better.

Song Index

Bile 'Em Cabbage Down 14
Blue Ridge Mountain Blues 32
Columbus Stockade Blues 28
Down the Road 16
Groundhog 18
Little Maggie 40
Long Journey Home 42
Lynchburg Town 20
Man of Constant Sorrow 56
My Home's Across the Blue Ridge Mountains 44
Nine Pound Hammer 26
Palms of Victory 24
Pass Me Not 46
Poor Ellen Smith 22
Pretty Polly 48
Put My Little Shoes Away 50
Red River Valley 38
Roll in My Sweet Baby's Arms 34
Shall We Gather at the River 52
Wabash Cannonball 36
When I Lay My Burden Down 30
When the Saints Go Marching In 54

Whew!

You've worked yourself through the book, and now you deserve a firm handshake, a pat on the head and a hardy congratulations. But before you faint of heatstroke basking in the glory of your many accomplishments, allow me to let a little air out of your balloon. You ain't done, not by any means. If you started out as a total ignoramus and you've gotten this far, you've learned a lot, no doubt. But now it's time to go back over the road you just traveled, this time mixing up your rolls, substituting one for another. You also need to get to the point where you aren't relying on this dumb book. The way to do that is to play the bare-bones skeleton of the tunes enough so you can play the basic tune without looking at the tablature. Then start adding the simplest rolls (starting with the pinch) and keep switching around your rolls until you get to the point where you play a tune differently each time you pick it. When you can do that, you've done something! Good luck, and let me hear from you with your successes and failures (if any!)

Native Ground Books & Music

Books of Songs, Instruction & Home Cookin'

Songbooks

Backpocket Bluegrass Songbook
Bluegrass Gospel Songbook
Cowboy Songs, Jokes, Lingo 'n Lore
Front Porch Songs, Jokes & Stories
Hymns of the Old Camp Ground
Outlaw Ballads, Legends, & Lore
Railroad Fever
Rousing Songs of the Civil War
Rural Roots of Bluegrass
Singing Rails

Instruction Books

Bluegrass Jamming on Banjo
Bluegrass Jamming on Fiddle
Bluegrass Jamming on Mandolin
Bluegrass Mandolin for the Complete Ignoramus!
Easy 2-Chord Songs for Guitar
Easy 2-Chord Songs for Mandolin
Flatpicking Guitar for the Complete Ignoramus!
Old-Time Fiddle for the Complete Ignoramus!
Painless Guitar
Ukulele for the Complete Ignoramus!

Nostalgic America

Log Cabin Pioneers
Manners & Morals of Victorian America
The Outhouse Papers

Home Cookin'

1st American Cookie Lady
A Garden Supper Tonight
Aunt Barb's Bread Book
Children at the Hearth
Early American Cookery
Log Cabin Cooking

Lost Art of Pie Making
Mama's in the Kitchen
Old-Time Farmhouse Cooking
Picnic Time!
Pioneer Village Cookbook
Secrets of the Great Old-Timey Cooks
Take Two & Butter 'Em While They're Hot!

Write or call for a FREE catalog
Native Ground Books & Music
109 Bell Road, Asheville, NC 28805
(828) 299-7031
banjo@nativeground.com
www.nativeground.com